AS Business Studies
UNIT 3
2ND EDITION

AQA

Module 3: External Influences and
Objectives and Strategy

John Wolinski

For my parents

Philip Allan Updates
Market Place
Deddington
Oxfordshire
OX15 0SE

Orders

Bookpoint Ltd, 130 Milton Park, Abingdon, Oxfordshire, OX14 4SB
tel: 01235 827720
fax: 01235 400454
e-mail: uk.orders@bookpoint.co.uk
Lines are open 9.00 a.m.–5.00 p.m., Monday to Saturday, with a 24-hour message answering service. You can also order through the Philip Allan Updates website: www.philipallan.co.uk

© Philip Allan Updates 2000
This edition © Philip Allan Updates 2003

ISBN-13: 978-0-86003-908-2
ISBN-10: 0-86003-908-0

This guide has been written specifically to support students preparing for the AQA AS Business Studies Unit 3 examination. The content has been neither approved nor endorsed by AQA and remains the sole responsibility of the author.

Printed by MPG Books, Bodmin

Contents

Introduction

About this guide 4

The aims of the AS qualification 5

Assessment 5

Preparation for Unit 3 — using the pre-issued case study 6

The skills requirement of a question 8

Opportunities for evaluation in Module 3 9

Revision strategies 9

■ ■ ■

Content Guidance

About this section 12

External Influences

Economic opportunities and constraints 13

Governmental opportunities and constraints 20

Social and other opportunities and constraints 22

Objectives and Strategy

Starting a small firm 26

Business objectives 30

Business strategy 34

■ ■ ■

Questions and Answers

About this section 38

Case study 1: External Influences — 'Jim's gym supplies' 39

Paper 1 Macroeconomic opportunities and constraints 43

Paper 2 The market and competition; governmental opportunities and
constraints; social and other opportunities and constraints 48

Case study 2: Objectives and Strategy — 'The everlasting sticky tape' 54

Paper 3 Starting a small firm 59

Paper 4 Business objectives and strategy 64

Case study 3: integrated case study for Units 2 and 3 — 'Double D delight' 72

Paper 5 Integrated Unit 2: People and Operations Management 78

Paper 6 Integrated Unit 3: External Influences and Objectives and Strategy 84

Introduction

About this guide

This Student Unit Guide has been written with one objective in mind: to provide you with the ideal resource for your revision of AQA Unit 3, AS Business Studies. After this introductory note on the aims and assessment of AS, the guide is divided into two sections: Content Guidance and Questions and Answers.

The first section offers concise coverage of Module 3, combining an overview of key terms and concepts with an identification of opportunities for you to illustrate the higher-level skills of analysis and evaluation. The scope for linking different topic areas is also shown.

The second section provides three pre-issued case studies, each accompanied by two sample examination papers with five questions in each. These are focused on a specific area of content and appear in the same order as the first section. In this way you can attempt an examination case study after studying or revising a specific part of the course, rather than wait until you have studied the whole specification.

Case study 1 is based on 'External Influences'. The information in this case study provides the background for Papers 1 and 2. Paper 1 focuses on macroeconomic opportunities and constraints and Paper 2 concentrates on the remaining external influences: market conditions and governmental, social, and other opportunities and constraints.

Case study 2 tests the 'Objectives and Strategy' element of the specification. Papers 3 and 4 are based on this case study. Paper 3 examines the issues surrounding starting a small firm, whilst Paper 4 contains questions on business objectives and strategy.

In the actual examination series (January and summer), the material in a pre-issued case study will be used to test both Unit 2 and Unit 3. To reflect this, Case study 3 provides the background for Papers 5 and 6 and has been designed to reflect the exact layout of questions in the AS examination. Paper 5 is an integrated 'People and Operations Management' examination. (Before attempting the questions you should read the Unit 2 student guide, to familiarise yourself with the content.) Paper 6 is an integrated 'External Influences and Objectives and Strategy' examination, covering all of the specification in Unit 3. Although it is possible to take Units 2 and 3 in different examination series, e.g. January and summer, this would mean that students would have to familiarise themselves with two separate case studies. AQA expects students to sit Units 2 and 3 (two 1-hour papers) in the same examination series, both in the same morning (or afternoon). It would be useful if Papers 5 and 6 were approached in this way.

You should read through the relevant topic area in the Content Guidance section before attempting the question from the Question and Answer section, and only read the specimen answers after you have tackled the question yourself.

The aims of the AS qualification

AS business studies aims to encourage candidates to:

- develop a critical understanding of organisations, the markets they serve and the process of adding value
- be aware that business behaviour can be studied from the perspectives of a range of stakeholders including customers, managers, creditors, owners/shareholders and employees
- acquire a range of skills, including those involved in decision-making and problem-solving
- be aware of current business structure and practice

Assessment

AS Unit 1 (Marketing and Accounting and Finance) is tested by a 1-hour data–response examination paper. Two questions, subdivided into four or five parts, are based on articles and data that are included in the examination paper.

For AS Unit 2 (People and Operations Management) and AS Unit 3 (External Influences and Objectives and Strategy), candidates will be given a pre-issued case study approximately 6 to 7 weeks before the date of the examination. On the day of the examination students will not be allowed to take their original copy into the examination, but will be issued with a clean copy along with the questions. Students will normally take two 1-hour papers based on the case study material (Units 2 and 3). After 1 hour the answers to Unit 2 will be collected in and the questions for Unit 3 handed out.

AS and A2 papers are designed to test certain skills. **Every mark that is awarded on an AS or A2 paper is given for the demonstration of a skill.** The content of the course (the theories, concepts and ideas) provides a framework which allows students to show their skills — recognising the content on its own is not enough to merit high marks.

The following skills are tested:

- **Knowledge and understanding** — recognising and describing business concepts and ideas.
- **Application** — being able to explain or apply your understanding.
- **Analysis** — developing a line of thought in order to demonstrate its impact or consequences.
- **Evaluation** — making a judgement by weighing up the evidence provided.

Unit 3 (External Influences and Objectives and Strategy) has a much higher weighting than Unit 1 (Marketing and Finance) for the higher-level skills of analysis and evaluation. However, its skills weighting is identical to Unit 2 (People and Operations Management). Bear this in mind during your preparation and revision for Unit 3, as you will need to practise developing arguments more fully for this paper in comparison to Unit 1. This will be good practice for A2 papers which, in general, have a higher weighting for these skills. The units have been designed to allow you to develop these skills as you progress through the course.

The weightings for this paper (and Unit 2) are the closest match to the overall weighting for the A-level (25% for each of the four different levels of skill). For this reason, on the basis of skills only, these two papers can be said to be the best guide to your overall performance in the A-level. However, a typical A-level student improves his or her skills during the 2 years of the course, and so the grade achieved at the end of the first year in this paper may not reflect the final grade accurately.

The examination papers for **Units 2 and 3** should be weighted so that marks for the paper as a whole are awarded approximately as follows:

Weighting

Knowledge   14/15   how well you know the meanings, theories and ideas
Application   14/15   how well you can explain benefits, problems, calculations, situations
Analysis   12   how well you develop ideas and apply theory and ideas to matters
Evaluation   9/10   how well you judge the overall significance of the situation

Total   50 marks

In addition, up to 3 marks are awarded in each unit for quality of language.

For reference purposes **Unit 1** (AS Marketing and Accounting and Finance) is weighted so that marks for the paper as a whole are awarded as follows:

Weighting

Knowledge   16/17   how well you know the meanings, theories and ideas
Application   16/17   how well you can explain benefits, problems, calculations, situations
Analysis   12   how well you develop ideas and apply theory and ideas to matters
Evaluation   5   how well you judge the overall significance of the situation

Total   50 marks

In this examination a maximum of 2 marks are awarded for quality of language.

Weighting of Units 1, 2 and 3
The relative weighting of the three units are:
Unit 1   30% of AS (15% of A-level)
Unit 2   30% of AS (15% of A-level)
Unit 3   40% of AS (20% of A-level)

Preparation for Unit 3 — using the pre-issued case study

Six or seven weeks before you sit the examination for Units 2 and 3 you will be issued with the case study (but not the questions). The case study will be quite detailed (approximately 2,500 words of text plus tables or charts of information).

When you receive the case study you should photocopy it. Use one copy as a working copy (keeping the other in a safe place in case you lose the first one). Read the case thoroughly prior to the examination in order to become familiar with the background, adding comments and notes as necessary. On the day of the examination you will not be able to take your copy of the case study into the examination room. You will be provided with a clean copy, along with a previously unseen examination paper. Do not rely on question spotting, as the case will be designed to cover a wide range of topics from the specification. Furthermore, the examiner may include additional (but brief) information within a question, to prevent you from anticipating all of the data that can be used. However, it is essential that you become thoroughly familiar with the situation in the case study. In a 1-hour examination it would be too time-consuming to keep referring back to the case. Consequently, the better your preparation and understanding, the easier it will be to answer the questions and manage your time.

Use the table below (produced by the Chief Examiner as a guide) as part of the planning process.

Analysing the pre-issued cases	
Key features of characters • What is their business experience? • What is their relationship? • Are they united (aims, leadership etc.)? • Do they seem calm under pressure? • Others (relevant to the case in question)?	**How is the business managed?** • Are the aims and objectives clear? • What is the style of leadership? • What is the business culture? • How are staff motivated? • Is it focused on stakeholders or shareholders?
Key characteristics of the business • Service or manufacturing? • Large or small, plc or Ltd? • Unlimited or limited liability? • Capital or labour intensive? • What are its main internal constraints?	**Key external influences of the business** • What is the income elasticity of the product/service? • Is it sensitive to any particular macro variables? • Does a firm face any particular social or ethical issues? • What market conditions does it face? (competition, excess capacity etc.)

Once you are familiar with the background, try to think of some questions that the examiner might ask. There are likely to be five questions. Two will require a definition and/or explanation of a term or concept; one will need analysis, whilst the other two will involve evaluation. (Remember that you will need to show knowledge, application and analysis within an evaluation question.) Although your questions may not match the final examination paper, you will find the process useful in trying to see how you might be tested and the level of detail that you may need to show. Most importantly, this activity will help you to become more knowledgeable about the case and so put your answers into a relevant context, enabling you to earn high marks for application and evaluation. (You may also make a lucky guess on a question!)

Practise the specimen questions included in the Question and Answer section of this unit guide. This should be included as a part of your revision plan and will help you to discover the different needs of this paper. Remember — give yourself plenty of time to familiarise yourself with the case study before you attempt one of the papers. In the 1 hour allowed you will not have enough time to refer back constantly to the whole of the case study.

The skills requirement of a question

A rough guide to the skills requirement of a question is its mark allocation. In the case of Unit 3, 53 marks are available (including 3 marks for quality of language). For individual questions the mark allocation is as follows:

4–6 marks   an explanation or calculation, showing **knowledge and application**

8–12 marks   development of an argument in the context of the question, showing **analysis**

14–16 marks   a judgement of a situation or proposed action, showing **evaluation**

In the assessment of higher-level questions requiring analysis or evaluation, marks will also be given for the other skills. Relevant factual information, for example, will earn marks for **knowledge**, whilst explanations and calculations will be awarded **application** marks.

An additional (and more useful) guide to the skills requirement of a question is to look at the trigger word introducing it. **Specific trigger words will be used to show you when you are being asked to analyse or evaluate.** For AS these will be restricted to the following:

Analyse
- 'Analyse...'
- 'Explain why...'
- 'Examine...'

Evaluate
- 'Evaluate...'
- 'Discuss...'
- 'To what extent...?'

If these trigger words are missing on an AS paper, you are being asked to show lower-level skills, i.e. knowledge of the specification content or application (explanation).

Students who fail to **analyse** generally do so because they have curtailed their argument. The words and phrases below serve to provide logical links in an argument.
- 'and so...'
- 'but in the long run...'
- 'which will mean/lead to...'
- 'because...'

By using them you can demonstrate your ability to analyse. Always ask yourself: 'am I explaining **why**?'

In order to **evaluate**, you need to demonstrate judgement and the ability to reach a reasoned conclusion. The following terms will demonstrate to the examiner that this is your intention:
- 'The most significant...is...because...'
- 'However, ...would also need to be considered because...'
- 'The probable result is...because...'

It is worth noting when studying for Unit 3 that questions involving the interpretation of numerate data and definition questions will be limited.

Within the specification, the main area that lends itself to interpretation of data is Section 12.1 on *Economic opportunities and constraints* which includes data on issues such as unemployment and inflation. Most of the other sections do not contain reference to issues that include numerate data, thus limiting the scope for numerate questions.

Although it is vital that you understand terms such as 'inflation', 'ethics' and 'SWOT', the fact that higher-level skills are being tested means that questions needing definitions will be limited.

Opportunities for evaluation in Module 3

The greater focus on evaluation in this module compared to the other two AS modules means that 25% of all marks are awarded for evaluation. Consequently, the specification provides many opportunities for both analysis and evaluation. Examples of these opportunities are listed at the end of each passage in the Content Guidance section of this book.

Module 3 incorporates some cross-referencing to elements of Modules 1 and 2 and this can lead to wide-ranging questions. Furthermore, business strategy is a very broad topic. Expect to be asked to judge the overall merits of a manager's decisions or to recommend a business strategy for a firm, based on the case study.

Revision strategies

Below is a list of general pieces of advice for exam preparation.
- Prepare well in advance.
- Organise your files, ensuring there are no gaps.
- Read different approaches — there is no one right approach to business studies. Experience as many views and methods as possible. Read newspapers and business articles.
- When reading an article, try to think of the types of question an examiner might ask and how you would answer them. Remember, some of your examination questions will be based on actual organisations.
- Take notes as you read. These will help you to:
  – put the text into your own words, cementing your understanding

– summarise and emphasise the key points

    – focus your attention

    – précis information which could help with future revision

    – boost your morale by showing an end product of your revision sessions

- Develop and use your higher-level skills. Make sure that your revision is not dominated by factual knowledge only. Check that you can explain and analyse the points noted, and try to imagine situations in which evaluation can be applied.
- Practise examination questions. Use the questions in this book (and past papers if available) to improve your technique, making sure that you complete them in the time allowed. In the examination you must complete all questions set on one case study in 60 minutes.
- Maintain your motivation. Reward yourself for achieving targets, but do not get demoralised if you fall behind. If necessary, amend your objectives to a more realistic level.
- Find out the dates and times of your examinations and use this to prepare a detailed schedule for the study leave/examination period, making sure you build in time for relaxation and sleep.
- Focus on all areas of the specification rather than just your favourite topics. Your revision is more likely to 'add value' if it improves your understanding of a problem area. Revising a topic that you already know is a morale booster, but is it as valuable?
- Top up your memory just before the examination. If there are concepts, formulae or ratios that you find difficult, revisit them just before the examination.
- Adopt your own strategy. Everyone has a different learning style — use one that works for you.

Content
Guidance

This section of the guide outlines the topic areas of Module 3 which are as follows:
- Economic opportunities and constraints
- Governmental opportunities and constraints
- Social and other opportunities and constraints
- Starting a small firm
- Business objectives
- Business strategy

Read through the relevant topic area before attempting a question from the Question and Answer section.

Key concepts

Key concepts are either defined or shown in bold. You should also have a business studies dictionary to hand.

Analysis

Under this heading there are suggestions on how topic areas could lend themselves to analysis. During your course and the revision period you should refer to these opportunities. Test and practise your understanding of the variety of ways in which a logical argument or line of reasoning can be developed.

Evaluation

Under this heading general opportunities for evaluation are highlighted within particular topic areas.

Integration

The AQA specification states that External Influences should be studied by looking at their influences on business decisions covered in Modules 1 and 2. Objectives and Strategy draw together all other modules, and should be seen as integrating themes which emphasise the interactive nature of the business world. Thus, all topics in Module 3 may need to be combined with elements from other AS modules.

Economic opportunities and constraints

The market and competition

Market conditions

The table shows the different types of competition within which businesses operate.

Feature	Perfect competition	Monopolistic competition	Oligopoly	Monopoly
Number of firms	Many	Many	Few	One *
Product	All the same	Differentiated	Differentiated	Unique
Example	Stock market	Insurance	Chocolate	Post Office — letters
Effect on business	Price takers. Cost efficiency needed for survival. No real scope for marketing. Very low profit margins. Easy to enter or leave the market.	Some influence on price. Cost efficiency very important. Low profit margins. Some benefit from marketing. Easy to enter or leave the market.	Non-price competition. High spending on promotion. High profit margins but higher overheads. Aim to achieve USPs through branding. Barriers to entry. Collusion between firms.	Will set price. High profit margins. Can become complacent. Attempt to maintain barriers to entry. Power will depend on importance of product/service and its alternatives.

* When investigating possible use of 'monopoly power', the government defines a monopoly as a firm with more than 25% of the market. This definition would apply to many oligopolists too.

Fair and unfair competition

The table shows that the more competitive the market, the less opportunity there is for profit. A general rule of thumb used by the government in investigating 'unfair competition' is the existence of 'supernormal' profit (profit that is well above the amount that could be 'reasonably expected').

'Unfair competition' is a subjective term. The award of a patent to a company guarantees it a monopoly for a number of years as a reward for the R&D undertaken. In this case, a high profit in one year may just be paying back costs from earlier years. Is it unfair to set a high price if people are prepared to pay it? The answer is more likely to be 'yes' for water supply than it is for a Manchester United shirt.

Examples of unfair competition

- Using an integrated product in a way that denies other companies the opportunity to compete (e.g. Microsoft using its Windows operating system to make it difficult for consumers to access other firms' Internet servers).
- A monopoly charging excessive prices because of the lack of competition.
- Oligopolists agreeing to restrict supply and fix high minimum prices.
- Market-sharing agreements — firms agreeing to operate as local monopolies by not challenging potential competitors in certain geographical areas.
- Restrictions on retailers, e.g. only supplying retailers if they guarantee not to stock rival products or only supplying if the retailer agrees to stock the complete range of a firm's products (full-line forcing).

The significance of the level of capacity in the market

Spare capacity in a market means that the maximum possible output of firms in the market exceeds the demand for the products.

Capacity shortage exists when the demand for the product exceeds the maximum possible supply/output of firms.

Spare capacity	Capacity shortage
• Low prices as companies need to sell their brands.	• High prices as demand exceeds supply.
• High fixed costs per unit, leading to higher average costs.	• Low fixed costs per unit and thus lower average costs.
• Lower profit margins.	• Higher profit margins.
• Restructuring of the company to dispose of surplus assets (e.g. labour or land).	• Investment programmes in order to acquire new fixed assets to increase capacity.
• Greater focus on marketing needed.	• Less need for marketing. Consolidation in existing market.
• Diversification into new markets.	• New firms entering the market.
• Firms leaving the market.	

Analysis Opportunities for analysis in this area include:
- assessing how profitability is affected by the market
- analysing factors that create certain market conditions
- comparing objectives and strategies under different market conditions
- assessing the causes or consequences of spare capacity/capacity shortage
- analysing situations involving possible examples of unfair competition

Evaluation Opportunities for evaluation in this area include:
- evaluating the implications of different market conditions for a firm's success
- judging the influence of market types on a firm's objectives and/or strategies
- discussing the significance of different factors that might be creating capacity shortage or spare capacity

- studying the impact of capacity shortage or spare capacity in a given case
- concluding whether competition is fair or unfair

Links Possible links to other areas include:
- Market conditions will have an impact on corporate aims and objectives.
- SWOT analysis (strengths, weaknesses, opportunities and threats) may be under-taken.
- The marketing mix may need to be adapted to the market situation (e.g. non-price competition in oligopoly markets).
- Product life cycle lengths will depend on the level of competition. In fact, most marketing strategies and tactics link to the market condition.
- Economies of scale will normally be more accessible for monopolists than firms in perfect competition, but less likely if spare capacity exists.

Macroeconomic issues — the business cycle and unemployment

The business cycle (or trade cycle)

The business cycle is the regular pattern of upturns and relative downturns in output and demand. A common description of the stages is shown in the diagram below.

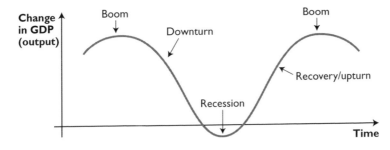

Potential causes of the cycle
- Changes in business confidence, leading to more dramatic changes in investment in fixed assets.
- Periods of stockbuilding or destocking.
- Government policies such as 'stop–go' which aim for growth prior to elections and necessitate applying anti-inflationary measures soon after them.
- Irregular patterns in consumer expenditure on durables influenced by factors such as security and confidence and interest rates.

The implications of the different stages (**boom**, **downturn**, **recession** and **recovery/upturn**) for the organisation are outlined overleaf.

Boom
- Demand exceeds supply ⟶ Prices rise
- Shortage of resources ⟶ Costs rise
- High capacity utilisation ⟶ New investment
- Overall increase in profit ⟶ High retained profits and dividends

Downturn
- Excess stocks ⟶ Need to cut some prices
- High inflation/costs ⟶ Reduces profit and confidence
- Government anti-inflation measures ⟶ Downturn in demand

Recession
- Fall in output and expenditure ⟶ Low profits or losses made
- Liquidations ⟶ Fewer suppliers or consumers
- Bad debts ⟶ Tighter credit control and thus less trade
- High unemployment ⟶ Switch in demand towards inferior goods
- Low investment ⟶ Disproportionate decline in capital goods firms

Recovery/upturn
- Rise in demand for consumer goods ⟶ Some increase in profit
- Time lag before capital investment ⟶ Uneven pace of recovery for different firms
- Business confidence growing ⟶ More investment; more borrowing
- Potential bottlenecks ⟶ High costs if there are shortages

Unemployment

Unemployment can be **cyclical** or **structural**.

Cyclical unemployment is caused by the overall fall in demand that tends to occur during the downturn or recession stages of the business cycle. The impact will vary according to the product or firm.
- Growth products are likely to overcome the effects of recession.
- Inferior goods may gain popularity as people cut back on luxuries.
- In theory, luxury products will decline for the above reason, although people who can afford luxuries are not so likely to become unemployed during a recession.
- Products on low profit margins may suffer as price becomes a more important element of the mix.
- Capital goods and construction firms are likely to experience the greatest problems as business confidence falls.

Structural unemployment is caused by demand or supply factors that apply to a particular industry. Examples include:
- the fall in demand for coal as it was replaced by other fuels
- UK textile firms failing to remain competitive due to low wages in other countries
- lack of competitiveness arising from other factors (e.g. poor reputation)
- technological changes

Implications of unemployment
- Consumer incomes fall, leading to lower sales and thus redundancies.
- Resource suppliers have weaker bargaining power and so raw material prices fall.
- Workers have less bargaining power as alternative jobs are harder to find, leading to lower wage levels.
- Cost-saving exercises will be undertaken, creating cost efficiencies but possible future problems through reduced training and wider spans of control.
- Cutbacks in investment for the future will lead to a further decline in employment.
- Diversification or takeovers and mergers may be used in order to rationalise.

Any desired change in policy may be threatened by the lack of finance available.

Analysis Opportunities for analysis of the trade cycle and unemployment include:
- examining the different causes of one or more stage of the business/trade cycle
- analysing the consequences of the business cycle stage on a particular organisation
- studying the impact of changing stock levels or capital investment or expenditure on consumer durables
- examining the different causes of unemployment in a particular situation
- analysing the implications of unemployment on a particular organisation
- showing how different elements/areas of a firm's activities (e.g. a product or department) may be influenced by unemployment

Evaluation Opportunities for evaluation include:
- judging the relative significance of the different causes of business cycle stages
- demonstrating how recession/boom etc. will have a different impact on different products or organisations
- assessing the relative significance of the different causes of unemployment in a particular situation

Links *Every* action taken by an organisation is directly or indirectly influenced by the business cycle or the level of unemployment. Booms create optimism in business planning; recessions tend to cause pessimism.

Macroeconomic issues — inflation, interest rates and exchange rates

Inflation

Inflation means an increase in price levels. (Deflation describes a decrease in price levels.)

The retail prices index
The retail prices index (RPI) measures inflation. Each month the government studies the prices of 'a typical cross-section of goods and services' that represent the spending

of an average family. The average price change (weighted to take into account the percentage of spend on each good) shows the rate of inflation (or deflation).

Causes of inflation

- **Demand** — if people are prepared to spend more money on products, then prices rise. This is usually caused by increases in consumers' incomes, but can also be the result of a willingness by customers to borrow more money.
- **Costs** — rising costs of raw materials, wages or other expenses result in companies increasing their prices in order to maintain profit levels.
- **Money supply** — prices rise if more money circulates without output rising.
- **Expectations** — if there is an expectation that prices will rise, demand will increase in the short term (before prices rise), so causing inflation. Consumers anticipating price rises will be more prepared to pay higher prices too.

Implications of inflation

- Higher prices may mean lower sales.
- The international competitiveness of UK firms will be reduced.
- Workers and suppliers will demand higher wages/prices.
- Future uncertainty will mean less reliable forecasts and plans.
- If the government or the Bank of England takes action it is likely to cause higher interest rates and pressure to cut demand and sales.
- Inflation encourages borrowing (but not if interest rates exceed inflation).

Interest rates

Interest rates show the cost of borrowing money, although they can also represent the reward paid for lending money. Loss of interest payments can therefore be seen as the opportunity cost of spending money.

Implications of a rise in interest rates

- Sales of products bought on credit will fall as repayments will be more expensive.
- Saving will be more attractive than spending, causing a further drop in sales.
- People with a mortgage will have less money. The UK has the second highest percentage of people with mortgages in Europe, so this effect is significant.
- There will be less investment for the future as the return on projects is less likely to exceed the interest payments that could be received.
- A rise in the cost of working capital will result in a desire to cut stocks.
- More international savings will be made in sterling to benefit from the interest rate, causing dearer exports but cheaper imports.

Exchange rates

The exchange rate is the price of one currency in terms of another. An **increase** in the exchange rate will result from the following:

- an increase in demand for a currency (caused by an **increase in exports**)
- a decrease in the supply of a currency (caused by a **decrease in imports**)

- high interest rates attracting savings from abroad
- speculation in favour of a currency (caused by speculators expecting a rise in value)
- foreign multinationals buying the currency in order to invest in that country
- governments buying that currency in order to support its value

Types of exchange rates

Flexible or **freely floating exchange rates** exist when the exchange rate is set by supply and demand (mainly based on imports and exports). Governments will not intervene to change the value. In theory, sterling is freely floating.

'Dirty' floating occurs when a floating exchange rate is influenced by government action in order to prevent it changing to an undesirable level.

Fixed exchange rates exist when the value of one currency is fixed against another. For example, 11 EU member countries fixed their exchange rates in preparation for the introduction of the euro on 1 January 1999.

Implications of changes in exchange rates

- An **increase** in the exchange rate means **dearer** exports but **cheaper** imports.
- A **decrease** in the exchange rate means **cheaper** exports but **dearer** imports.
- **Any change** in exchange rates makes it impossible for a company to predict the volume or the price received from its overseas transactions. This discourages trade as it increases the level of risk. Buying currency in advance at a guaranteed, fixed rate helps, but this costs money and therefore reduces profits.

Note: exports and imports also depend on other factors, including reputation and quality, after-sales service and the reliability, design and desirability of the product, the overall package provided and payment terms.

Analysis Opportunities for analysis in this area include:
- demonstrating the causes of inflation
- showing how inflation affects a particular organisation's policies
- examining the reasons for a change in interest rates
- studying the implications of changes in interest rates on an organisation
- analysing the implications of fixed and/or flexible exchange rates
- showing how exchange rate changes affect an organisation

Evaluation Opportunities for evaluation include:
- recognising how price elasticity of demand will influence the effect of inflation
- discussing how the cause of inflation can have different implications for a company
- evaluating how interest rate changes affect durable goods, such as cars and furniture, more than smaller items that are not bought on credit
- evaluating the significance of exchange rate changes according to whether the firm is an exporter or importer; the importance of price relative to other factors; the percentage of company activity involving trade; which countries it trades with (the pound may be rising against one currency but falling in value against another)

Governmental opportunities and constraints

UK and EU law

The focus here is on:

- **The reasons for legislation.** In general terms legislation in this area is intended to:
  - protect those with weaker bargaining power, e.g. employees in a large firm or small firms negotiating with a large, powerful trade union
  - ensure that UK firms meet the needs of customers in a cost-effective way which leads to international competitiveness
- **The implications of legislation.** Legislation reduces the possibility of a firm exploiting its customers through unfair activities. It also allows governments to ensure that social factors (externalities) are considered in decision-making. Higher prices (but better products) may result from the legislation.

Health and safety

The aim of health and safety legislation is to provide a safe working environment for employees. The Health and Safety at Work Act (1974) provides the basis and states that firms must provide a safe environment, a written safety policy and training. However, employees must take responsibility for their own and others' safety.

EU directives control working hours, workers lifting heavy weights or using computer screens, and the rights of pregnant workers.

Implications of health and safety legislation

- Extra costs — safety measures, training and employment of safety staff.
- Reputation — a lack of safety could damage sales and recruitment.
- Motivation — security is seen as a factor that can avoid demotivation.

Employment

Employment protection falls into two categories: **individual employment law** and **collective labour law**.

Individual employment law

This legislation aims to ensure that employers and employees act fairly in dealing with others. Key legislation includes:

- Equal Pay Act, 1970
- Sex Discrimination Acts, 1975 and 1986
- Race Relations Act, 1976
- Disability Discrimination Act, 1995

Collective labour law

This legislation aims to control industrial relations and trade union activities. Various pieces of legislation cover the following:

- Contracts of employment — employees must receive a contract within 13 weeks if employed for more than 16 hours per week.
- Notice of dismissal — after 4 weeks of work an employee is guaranteed 1 week's notice, increasing to 1 week for every year employed up to a maximum of 12 weeks.
- Dismissal procedures — all employees must be told about the formal procedures that must be followed by the company.
- Trade union activities, e.g. rules on picketing and strikes.

Consumer protection

Consumer protection legislation aims to safeguard consumers from exploitation or exposure to unsafe products or services. Legislation, overseen by the Office of Fair Trading (OFT), includes:

- Sale of Goods Act, 1979 — goods must be fit for the particular purpose, of merchantable quality, as described.
- Weights and Measures Act, 1963 and 1985 — weights and measures must be accurate and displayed.
- Trade Descriptions Act, 1968 — adverts must be truthful and accurate.
- Consumer Credit Act, 1974 — limits the giving of credit to licensed brokers/organisations.
- Consumer Protection Act, 1987 — companies are responsible for damage caused by their products.
- Food Safety Act, 1990 — controls the safety of food products.

In addition there are voluntary controls, monitored by the industry or through an independent body such as the Advertising Standards Authority (ASA).

Implications of consumer protection

- Increased costs of production.
- Potential savings on rectifying problems.
- Improved quality and thus enhanced reputation and consumer loyalty.

Competition policy

This aims to limit the power of firms to take advantage of monopolies, mergers and restrictive practices. Competition should lead to better quality, cheaper products and to increasing international competitiveness.

Ways of safeguarding against such exploitation include:

- The Competition Commission — this body ensures that firms with a significant market share (or proposed mergers) do not act against consumers' interests.

- Watchdog organisations such as OFWAT and OFGAS — these were set up to prevent privatised companies from exploiting their customers.
- Greater competition — forcing government bodies to contract out services to the best bid, in order to prevent excessive pricing and poor service.
- Reducing restrictive practices — taking measures to prevent actions (such as cartels) that limit competition and customer choice.

Implications of competition policy

- Lower prices for customers.
- Lower profit margins for companies.
- Greater incentives for firms to seek competitive advantage through 'fair' rather than 'unfair' competition (e.g. by creating cheaper or innovative products).

Analysis Opportunities for analysis include:
- investigating the reasons for government legislation
- showing how a company needs to adapt its strategy to a change in legislation
- analysing the impact of government actions on an organisation or particular situation
- examining the pros or cons of an area of government or EU law

Evaluation Opportunities for evaluation include:
- evaluating the relative merits of different forms of legislation
- discussing the impact of laws on a particular organisation
- arguing the overall case for government intervention of this type

Social and other opportunities and constraints

Social responsibilities

Social responsibilities are the firm's duties towards society in the form of stakeholders. The key requirements of the various stakeholders are summarised below.

Stakeholders	Key requirement of stakeholder
Employees	Secure, reasonably paid employment.
Customers	Good quality, safe products at a competitive price.
Suppliers	Fair prices and regular custom and payment.
Owners	Good profit leading to increases in share prices and/or dividends.
Government/society	Efficient use of resources and also consideration of the environment and society's needs.
Local community	Employment and wealth creation without imposing major social costs.

From the firm's perspective, being socially responsible has the following benefits:
- It improves image, meaning higher sales.
- It encourages greater brand loyalty, allowing higher prices.
- It makes it easier to recruit the best workers and motivate staff.

A firm which accepts its social responsibilities can face the following problems:
- Socially responsible policies can be costly to introduce.
- A culture change within the company may be necessary.
- Adopting these policies will cause conflict between stakeholders.
- Social costs and benefits are not always easy to identify, e.g. Monsanto saw GM crops as a way of eliminating the problems of plant disease.

The table below sets out **the arguments for and against social responsibilities**.

Arguments for	Arguments against
• Problems such as unemployment and pollution will be reduced.	• The efficient use of resources may be reduced if businesses are restricted in how they can produce and where they can locate. This will cause higher prices.
• The quality of life will be improved as decisions will be based on what is best for society rather than what is best for one firm.	• International competitiveness will be reduced if other countries do not consider externalities.
• Business wealth can be used to help society.	• Stakeholders will always have different views.
• Morally, individual organisations should do the right thing.	• Social responsibility is subjective and is much harder to measure than clear profit targets.
• Society's long-term needs can be considered when a business might focus only on the short term.	• Business managers may lack the skills to deal with such issues.

Business ethics

Ethical behaviour is subjective. In broad terms, ethical behaviour is behaviour that is seen to be morally correct. Examples of ethical issues include:
- Should a firm relocate to a country paying lower wage levels?
- Should a firm release a life-saving drug after limited testing?
- Should private health care organisations train doctors and nurses?
- Can organisations, such as Railtrack, balance profit and safety?
- Should companies practise positive discrimination?
- Should advertising aimed at children be restrained?
- Should working hours be limited?

The pros and cons of ethical behaviour are similar to those shown under social responsibilities (above). A further issue is the implementation of an ethical policy.

The following points highlight the possible **difficulties** firms could face when deciding whether to adopt an ethical policy.

- **Effect on profit** — an ethical choice can incur extra costs, e.g. buying renewable resources from a less developed country; continuing extensive testing of a product before release; failing to introduce products that do not meet ethical standards.
- **What is ethical?** People have different views on what is ethical and these change over time. An example of this in Britain is Sunday trading.
- **Communication of ethics within the organisation** — in large organisations it may be difficult to inform staff of the policy and to monitor adherence to it.
- **Delegation and empowerment** — as empowered workers take more decisions, it becomes harder to maintain a company policy on ethical behaviour.

Analysis Opportunities for analysis in this area include:
- examining the level of social responsibility shown by a firm
- showing how a more socially responsible (or ethical) policy can be implemented
- analysing why a firm might want to become more (or less) socially responsible
- demonstrating the consequences of a particular ethical or socially influenced decision
- analysing the conflict between profit and ethics
- showing how different stakeholders take varying stances on these issues
- examining the impact of delegation on ethical decision-making

Evaluation Opportunities for evaluation in this area include:
- making a judgement on the key social/moral issues influencing policy
- assessing the desirability of balancing social and other needs
- evaluating the impact of different stakeholder needs
- monitoring the extent to which social and ethical decisions depend on other factors such as the market and competition
- contrasting the short-term and long-term implications of social responsibility

Technological change

Technology is constantly advancing. Areas of technological change include products and services, production processes, operating methods and materials.

The **benefits** from new technology to society, firms and consumers are:
- **Improved efficiency and reduced waste** — cost-effective use of the world's resources benefits consumers and firms, and in the long run resources last longer.
- **Better products and services** — company profits are increased and consumers benefit from better choice.
- **New products and materials** — needs and wants that were previously not satisfied are provided for.
- **Advances in communication** — company efficiency is increased and consumer needs are met more directly.
- **Improved working environments** — employees work in safer conditions and there

are greater numbers of jobs which are less physically demanding and more interesting.
- **Wealth creation** — higher living standards are achieved.

The **problems** of introducing new technology are:
- **Cost** — the need to remain up to date can lead to very high replacement costs on a more regular basis.
- **Knowing when and what to buy** — in rapidly changing markets, an investment in technology that is about to be dated can be an expensive mistake.
- **Industrial relations** — with technology replacing jobs there is a danger of resistance by workers and a lowering of morale.
- **Personnel** — new skills are required with implications for recruitment, retention and training costs.
- **Breakdowns** — where processes become dependent on technology, breakdowns can cause major disruption and therefore expense.

Firms may experience **resistance to changes** in technology for a number of reasons:
- Some people have a natural tendency to resist change.
- Employees may recognise that individually they will suffer from a change, even if the firm as a whole benefits.
- Employees may not recognise the benefits (they may have received no explanation).
- Stakeholders will view the implications differently. For example, a customer might see a better product, whilst the local community might see job losses.
- Workers can have different values. One worker may value the improved pay; another may regard the lower job security as more significant.

Analysis This area lends itself to an analysis of the extent of the benefits to a business. As new technology (unless restricted by a patent) is available to all organisations, the benefit depends on the degree to which competitors can match the firm.

Products
- In the short term, benefits arising from new products may be very significant. Consumers will pay premium prices for a unique product.
- This 'supernormal' profit can remain if a patent can prevent competition. However, there will probably be 'me-too' products that reduce the uniqueness of the original.
- Companies can use this period to develop the next, unique product.
- In a monopolistic market, the lack of competition will allow companies to continue to make high profits, thus limiting the incentive to introduce new, improved products.
- In some industries the high cost of new technology acts as a barrier to entry, allowing organisations to keep profit high in the long run.

Processes
- New technology can improve the efficiency of processes. In the short term, this may help a company to raise its profit margins.
- In a competitive market this advantage will soon disappear as new firms adopt these processes too, causing margins to decrease.

- In the long run, the profit will rise through greater sales volume as the lower price will make the product accessible to more customers.

Other issues for analysis in this area could relate to the following points:

- The adoption of new technology will be influenced by existing technology. Is it compatible? Can the changeover in methods be managed?
- Reaction of the workforce to new technology — the cooperation of employees will be needed.
- Stress — any change brings with it a period of stress and companies need to monitor the signs of stress if they wish to ensure a smooth transition.

Evaluation This topic lends itself to evaluation as a range of issues can be introduced. In any given scenario there needs to be a reasoned judgement balancing the benefits of new technology (usually new markets and customers) against the problems created (usually personnel and operational issues). Other considerations are finance (problems in the short term but benefits in the long term) and the reliability of projections. It is impossible to be totally sure of the impact of change.

Starting a small firm
Identifying an opportunity

Given that approximately one third of all new businesses fail in their first 3 years, an entrepreneur has to think carefully about the logic behind a new business. Business opportunities can take a number of forms:

- **Using existing skills** — a firm based on the existing skills and understanding of the owner should benefit from this individual's awareness of the market and interest in the tasks. The main problems are likely to be the marketability of the idea.
- **Identifying a gap in the market** — assuming the firm attracts sufficient customers, does the owner have the necessary skills to meet their needs profitably?
- **Purchasing a franchise** — this is a tried and tested idea which limits the risk of the owner. However, it also limits profitability and the franchisee may be vulnerable if the franchisor has not researched the possibility carefully.
- **Invention or innovation** — inventors who start a firm on the strength of a new invention have the benefit of a market niche but the possible problem of being product-led rather than market-led.

Protecting ideas

The methods below allow a firm to retain its unique appeal by preventing direct copying. However, for very small firms the costs may be too high.

- **Patents** — provide inventors with exclusive rights to make a product for 16 to 20 years.

- **Registered design** — a form of protection which prevents copy of designs for a period of up to 15 years.
- **Trademarks** — indicated by the symbol ®. They take the form of a symbol or style of wording that cannot be copied by rivals.
- **Copyright** — indicated by the symbol ©. It applies to printed material such as a book that cannot be copied directly.

Research and marketing with small budgets

Research can be carried out using the following methods and resources:
- the _Yellow Pages_ or local business directories to show what is offered and where
- market mapping — this can show a gap in the market for a product or service that is not being provided at all
- other secondary sources — census data or local government data
- primary research — limited direct research or information gleaned from listening to local people (e.g. complaints about leaky garage roofs on a particular estate)

Marketing can be carried out via the following:
- leaflet distribution personally or through a local newspaper or distributor
- posters in shop windows
- advertisements in the local newspaper, possibly with special offers
- local business directories or the _Yellow Pages_
- specialist magazines relevant to the product (these may be national)
- public relations (PR) — arranging events that will achieve newspaper coverage
- word-of-mouth — comments from satisfied customers are a major form of marketing for a new firm

Practical problems of start-up

The potential problems that start-ups can encounter are shown in the table below.

Finance	Marketing	Operational	Personnel	Personal
• raising funds • cash flow • profitability • investment	• deciding on the product • forecasting sales • target market • market research • price competition • forms of promotion	• suitable premises • location • production methods • sources of supply	• recruitment • selection • training • structure	• suitability for self-employment • cover for illness • opportunity cost

Analysis Opportunities for analysis include:

- examining the qualities needed by an entrepreneur
- analysing the marketability of the product or service
- considering the importance of other internal issues that determine success
- analysing the impact of external factors
- assessing the feasibility, advantages or weaknesses of a business plan

Evaluation This topic lends itself to evaluation. Scenarios can be created in which a number of factors will determine the success or failure of a business start-up. Evaluation may consider:

- why a start-up failed
- how well a start-up was managed
- why a new business succeeded
- the measures that a firm should take
- the degree to which the owner might have influenced failure (or success)
- starting a manufacturing firm as opposed to a tertiary organisation

Legal structure

Limited or unlimited liability?

There are two broad categories of business, **incorporated** and **unincorporated**.

Unincorporated

In an **unincorporated** business there is no distinction in law between the individual owners of a business and the business itself. Such businesses are in the hands of sole traders or partnerships. *(No understanding of partnerships is required for the AQA A-level in business studies.)*

In the eyes of the law, an individual must pay his or her debts to any creditors in full. This concept is known as **unlimited liability**. Any debts that the business owes must be paid out of the funds of the owner.

Incorporated

An **incorporated** business has a legal identity that is separate from the individual owners. In the private sector these are private limited companies (Ltds), public limited companies (PLCs) and cooperatives, mutuals or friendly societies. *(No understanding of cooperatives, mutuals or friendly societies is required for the AQA A-level in business studies.)* These firms can own assets, owe money and enter into contracts in their own right as they are recognised legally as a separate entity.

A feature of incorporated businesses is **limited liability**. The liability of these firms is limited to the fully paid-up share capital. So, if the business goes into liquidation the owners (shareholders) have no responsibility for further payments if they have already paid for their shares. Legally the business has 'died' and so its debts 'die' with it.

Forms of business ownership

The forms of business ownership covered by AS are:

Sole trader — a business owned by one person. He or she may employ staff. Sole traders are most commonly found in the provision of local services.

Private limited company (Ltd) — funded by shares that cannot be advertised for sale without the agreement of the other shareholders. This means that second-hand shares cannot be sold on the stock exchange. As a result, they are limited in size.

Public limited company (PLC) — funded by shares. PLCs must issue at least £50,000 of shares, and their shares can be advertised. Most try to secure a stock exchange listing allowing their second-hand shares to be bought and sold easily.

The **advantages and disadvantages** of these types of businesses are shown below.

Type of business	Advantages	Disdvantages
Sole trader	• Easy and cheap to set up. • Very flexible to changes in circumstances. • Owner takes all of the profit (and thus there is strong motivation). • Independence. • More privacy than other firms.	• Unlimited liability. • High risk and limited collateral for loans. • Limited capital. • Organisational difficulties (holidays and illness). • Limited skills.
Private limited company	• Limited liability. • More capital than sole traders. • More privacy than PLCs. • More flexible than PLCs.	• Shares less attractive because they are difficult to sell. • Less flexible if expansion needs finance. • Legal formalities compared to unincorporated firms.
Public limited company	• Limited liability. • Easier to raise finance. • Greater scope for new investment. • Can obtain economies of scale. • Stock exchange listing acts as a guarantee of stability.	• Must publicise performance. • Greater scrutiny of activities. • More administration. • Founders of firm may lose control of ownership.

The divorce between ownership and control

Traditionally entrepreneurs have two functions:
(1) taking risks (by providing finance) — **ownership**
(2) making decisions (managing the organisation) — **control**

In a sole trader business, the owner and manager are likely to be the same person so these functions remain with that one person (the entrepreneur).

However, in PLCs, the owners (shareholders) vote for directors who appoint managers to make the decisions. In this case, the two functions of ownership and control are divorced (separated). These functions have become split because:

- The growth of firms has led to many limited companies expanding beyond their original owners (e.g. a Ltd company becoming a PLC) in order to compete.
- Large PLCs have attracted shareholders who only wish to earn dividends or capital gains but do not want to be involved in management.
- Additional wealth has led to more people acquiring the finances needed to purchase shares.
- Deliberate government policy has widened share ownership.

However, two trends have limited the extent of this divorce:
(1) The growth of small firms in recent years.
(2) The decline of public ownership.

Implications of a divorce
- It is easier for companies to acquire more finance.
- Managers can be selected on merit rather than share ownership.
- There is a greater conflict of interests, with managers taking decisions that may not suit the needs of the owners.
- Shareholders find it difficult to access the information needed to challenge or judge the quality of managers' decisions.
- Shareholders take a narrow focus on short-term finances as they have less understanding of the needs of other stakeholders.

> **Analysis and evaluation** The descriptive nature of this element limits the scope for analysis and evaluation. The main opportunities exist in contrasting the relative merits of different forms of ownership (particularly the choice facing a person in a given situation); commenting on the merits of limited liability; and evaluating the causes or implications of the divorce between ownership and control.

Business objectives

Corporate aims and goals

Corporate aims

These are the long-term intentions of an organisation. The aims, sometimes in the form of a **mission statement**, provide a general focus from which more specific objectives can be set.

Corporate objectives (or goals)

These are medium- or long-term goals that provide a more measured, specific translation of the aims, allowing an organisation to measure the level of achievement of its aims. The **purposes of objectives** are to:
- provide direction

- unify staff
- measure and improve efficiency
- motivate staff
- pinpoint strengths and weaknesses and allow action to be taken
- monitor the relevance of activities
- communicate to stakeholders

Good objectives will be **SMART**:

Specific   **M**easurable   **A**ttainable   **R**ealistic   **T**imed

Typical corporate objectives are laid out in the table below.

Objective	Analysis
Survival	A key objective for most small or new firms.
	More significant during periods of uncertainty and recession.
	Important in competitive markets.
Financial	Profit-maximising in theory, but more likely to be satisficing (a satisfactory level of profit).
	Short-term profit may conflict with long-term profit.
	Break-even will be the target for mutual societies, friendly societies and public services.
	Profit target must be adjusted to the business environment and so it will be influenced by the level of competition, existence of spare capacity, stage of the business cycle, demand for the product etc.
Growth	A popular objective because it is easy to measure.
	Less likely for small businesses that value independence.
	Affected by the external factors noted above.
Corporate image (reputation and image/product quality)	Pride of the owners may lead to this being a key objective.
	Likely to help other objectives such as growth and profit.
	Will vary according to the customers' needs — a quality image will appeal to consumers who buy on the basis of quality rather than price.
	Image depends on the market segment — 'cheap and cheerful' may be the best reputation in a certain market.
	The level of competition will affect the need for a positive image.
Meeting the needs of other stakeholders	Many organisations place a high value on considering the needs of others in their corporate objectives (this can also enhance reputation).
	Examples are: • providing good working conditions, pay, opportunities and training for workers • environmental priorities — ensuring that products and processes do not damage the environment • social awareness — providing for the needs of the local community and disadvantaged sectors of society

Long-term or short-term objectives

Objective-setting can be seen as an early stage in business decision-making. Decisions need to be made in the context of the firm's overall aims. However, in practice, objectives are constantly modified in the light of market changes, levels of achievement and future opportunities.

In general, the achievement of long-term aims will be a dominant influence on a company's actions. On occasion, short-term objectives may vary from the long-term aims for the following reasons:

- **Financial crisis** — this will encourage a firm to look towards survival rather than growth or profit.
- **New competition** — long-term needs might encourage a firm to modify its policy in order to eliminate a rival. For example, destroyer (or predator) pricing might be used for a short time until the competition is eliminated and price can be increased again.
- **Economic conditions** — in a recession, greater emphasis will be placed on survival; in a boom, the potential for high profits may encourage other targets, such as helping the environment or local community, or diversification.
- **Government policy** — changes (e.g. in employment policy) may force a company to adopt different priorities.
- **Image changes** — negative publicity may encourage a firm to focus on improving its image in the short term in order to re-establish itself in the market.
- **Management style** — the owner may prefer to focus on the immediate future.

Analysis The table on page 31 highlights the factors that influence the actual objectives chosen by an organisation. Further potential for analysis includes:

- examining the reasons for objectives
- considering reasons for adopting short-term objectives
- analysing the quality of a specific objective
- recommending suitable objectives for a given organisation
- showing the links between objectives and company policies
- looking at the implications for companies/departments of switching between short-term and long-term objectives

Evaluation Opportunities for evaluation include:

- demonstrating the degree to which objectives are appropriate to a firm
- evaluating the different influences on a firm's objectives
- judging the actions of a company in the context of its objectives
- discussing the merits and suitability of an organisation's objectives
- evaluating the relative merits of short- and long-term objectives in a particular situation
- judging the importance of *agreed* objectives in a specific organisation

Stakeholders

Traditionally, firms were established by their owners to meet the needs of those owners. Business aims and objectives were therefore dominated by the needs of the shareholders (the owners). This approach is known as the **shareholder concept**.

Over the years, a number of organisations took a different view by prioritising the needs of other groups (e.g. the John Lewis Partnership meeting the needs of employees; the Cooperative Society satisfying customer needs). Governments have also restricted corporate decisions in order to meet the wider needs of society by considering externalities arising from those decisions. Theorists, notably Charles Handy, have supported the view that firms should take the initiative in meeting the needs of these other **stakeholders**.

A stakeholder is an individual or group with an interest in an organisation's performance.

Common and conflicting aims

A company should try to serve the needs of these groups or individuals, but whilst some needs are common, other needs conflict.

Even within a stakeholder group there may be conflicting aims — some customers will favour low prices whilst others will favour quality. The list below summarises the possible requirements of each stakeholder group in terms of their objectives.

Shareholders
- high profit secured by cheap costs or high prices
- high dividends
- long-term growth to support share prices
- cost-effective production
- positive corporate image

Staff (workforce)
- job security
- good working conditions
- high pay
- labour-intensive production

Customers
- low prices
- high-quality products
- good service
- invention and innovation
- choice

Suppliers
- regular custom, prompt payment and reasonable prices for materials
- growth, leading to more orders in the future

Residents
- employment prospects
- safeguarding the environment
- acceptance of social costs such as noise and water pollution

The state
- employment
- reasonable prices
- efficient use of resources
- compliance with legislation on consumer protection and competition policy
- compliance with legislation on employment and health and safety

  Analysis Opportunities for analysis include:
  - explaining how and why different stakeholders listed above would prioritise their aims
  - demonstrating the common aims of different stakeholder groups
  - analysing the conflict between the aims of different groups
  - assessing the impact on a company changing from the 'shareholder concept' to a consideration of all stakeholder needs
  - explaining how a company benefits from serving the needs of different stakeholders

  Evaluation Opportunities for evaluation include:
  - discussing the relative importance of different stakeholders in a particular case
  - evaluating the circumstances in which the views of individual groups will be considered
  - judging the degree of common ground and/or conflict between different aims
  - evaluating the types of aims or objectives that a firm should pursue in order to meet its stakeholder needs
  - discussing the impact of a decision/event on specific stakeholders

Business strategy

SWOT analysis

SWOT analysis is a system that allows an organisation to assess its overall position, or the position of one of its divisions, products or activities. The analysis looks at the **internal factors** within the company that influence its position. These are:
- **S**trengths
- **W**eaknesses

External factors that might influence the position of a business are described as:

- **O**pportunities
- **T**hreats

Areas that could be assessed in a SWOT analysis vary from organisation to organisation, but some aspects that are likely to be included are outlined below.

Internal factors

- reputation or corporate image
- quality of product
- level of innovation
- brands and product portfolio
- understanding of the market
- skills of personnel
- recruitment, selection and training
- attitudes and turnover of staff
- fixed assets and investment
- research and development levels
- location
- company structure
- operational methods
- profitability
- liquidity

External factors

- stage of the business cycle
- local economic conditions
- degree and type of competition
- actions of competitors
- developments within the market
- government economic policy
- legislation
- accessibility of new markets
- extent of change
- technology
- social and political trends
- demographic changes
- pressure group activity

SWOT analysis is the application of these and other factors to a particular organisation (or element of that organisation) in order to assist planning. An example of a SWOT analysis drawing on the internal and external factors above is shown in the table overleaf.

Internal factors	
Strengths	**Weaknesses**
Excellent reputation for high-quality products.	Reputation as a poor employer.
High-quality products.	Product portfolio has too many products in decline and growth stages, with a shortage of products in maturity.
Seen as innovative.	Expertise in a limited range of market segments.
Highly skilled staff, selected through a well-organised recruitment process.	Limited provision of training for office staff and production line workers.
Sound investment in fixed assets and modern equipment and methods.	High levels of staff turnover and absenteeism.
An international leader in research and development in its field.	Poor accessibility to location of main headquarters.
An efficient, delayered company structure.	Communication difficulties between different divisions and subsidiaries.
Very profitable in comparison to similar organisations.	Low level of liquidity; cash flow problems in recent years.

External factors	
Opportunities	**Threats**
Low wages and high unemployment levels for local people with appropriate skills.	Downturn predicted in the business cycle.
Main competitor experiencing financial difficulties.	High levels of competition within the market.
Government economic policy is encouraging more spending.	Many new products are being released by new entrants into the market.
Recent legislation will require many companies to buy one of the industry's pieces of equipment.	Technological changes mean that recent capital purchases will become obsolete soon.
New markets opening up in other parts of the world.	An ageing population will mean fewer sales of certain products.
Social trends will encourage families to purchase more of certain products.	Pressure group activity against the opening of a new factory.

Evaluation Although SWOT is described as analysis, it also involves evaluating the relative importance of the causes and/or consequences of the strengths, weaknesses, opportunities and threats.

Questions
&
Answers

In this section of the guide there are three case studies, each providing the background information for two examination papers; a total of six question papers in all. Each question paper is followed by two sample answers interspersed with examiner's comments.

Questions

The questions are based on the format of the AS papers. This unit (External Influences and Objectives and Strategy) is based on a lengthy pre-issued case study that you will receive approximately 6–7 weeks before the examination. In the exam, time will be precious and so **it is essential that you enter the examination room knowing as much about the situation in the case study as possible.** The questions will require you to apply your business understanding to the case and so you will be given a clean copy. Do refer to the case study during the examination where necessary — it is unlikely that you will be able to remember every detail.

Tackle the questions in this book to develop your technique, allowing yourself 60 minutes to answer all parts of each question paper. Ideally, set aside 2 hours and answer both papers connected to a given case study at the same time. However, if you have only revised a specific area of the specification it would be more useful to do them one at a time. By considering the specimen answers provided and the examiner's comments, you will be able to see how these questions may be answered effectively and identify (and so avoid) the potential pitfalls.

A common problem for students (and teachers) when completing a topic is the lack of examination questions that cover only the topic in question. These questions have been tailored so that students can apply their learning whilst a topic is still fresh in their minds. **Papers 1 to 4** are focused on a specific area of content. These questions may be tackled during the course or on completion of the revision of that particular content area. **Case study 3 (Paper 6)** is integrated, covering the whole of the Module 3 content in the way that the final examination will. The AQA pre-issued case study is also designed to be the background for Unit 2, so each case study contains references to issues from Module 2. To reflect the real examination, **Paper 5** is a Unit 2 examination paper, based on Case study 3. (The Unit 2 guide includes an integrated Unit 3 paper in the same way.)

Sample answers

Resist the temptation to study the answers before you have attempted the questions. In each case, the first answer (by Candidate A) is intended to show the type of response that would earn a grade A on that paper. An A grade does not mean perfection — these answers are intended to show the range of responses that can earn high marks. Candidate B's answers demonstrate responses that contain common errors.

Examiner's comments

The examiner's comments are preceded by the icon *e*. They are interspersed in the answers and indicate where credit is due. In the weaker answers, they also point out areas for improvement, specific problems and common errors.

Jim's gym supplies

Jim Stevenson, the founder and managing director of SMET, paused for a moment to consider the excited comments of Emily Duport, the marketing manager. 'Emily, I agree that this idea looks like a winner, and that we need to keep researching different markets, but we are in danger of spreading ourselves too thin.'

(A) The early years

Jim had founded SMET in 1970. He had spotted a gap in the market for mass-produced small engineering parts. At the time, other engineering firms were focusing increasingly on large-scale parts, ignoring the demand for nuts, bolts, nails and other small metal products. However, 33 years later, the original factory (now the engineering components division of SMET) was finding it tough. Its market was populated by hundreds of small firms, all producing identical components for the machine tool industry. Furthermore, the relatively simple manufacturing processes meant that only unskilled labour was needed to make the components and that the machines needed were easy and cheap to purchase. More and more of SMET's former customers were purchasing from Asia and eastern Europe, where labour costs and land rents were much lower.

At first SMET had reacted by emphasising the quality of its products. The new system had taken a long time to introduce. The workforce had been opposed to the new techniques that were needed. The shift from a standard style of flow production to cell production had not been easy. The workers resented the time spent on their retraining. The culture was such that the workers disliked taking responsibility — it was always useful to have the quality inspectors to blame if things went wrong. However, under the new system of cell production, each cell was responsible for its own production rate and for guaranteeing high quality. When a 'total quality management' system was introduced, there was no longer any need for an inspection team — 'right first time' was the new motto.

It took some time for the new system to settle — a time during which there were frequent industrial disputes, high absenteeism and low productivity. As a result, even more customers were lost to the cheap imports flooding in from Asia and eastern Europe.

(B) Diversification

Fortunately for SMET, Emily Duport, the marketing manager, had persuaded the board in 1987 to diversify into the manufacture of fitness equipment. This had seemed an unlikely market at the time. Jogging was all the rage and budget-conscious local councils that operated the local sports centres purchased most fitness equipment.

Emily, however, had anticipated the growth and popularity of private gyms and health clubs. As the 'first mover' in this market, SMET had met with considerable success. The scope for selling goods with high 'value added' had attracted Jim. For nuts, bolts and the other small components there were very low profit margins, but one exercise treadmill could generate as much profit as a huge number of nails or screws. Even now, 15 years after SMET had diversified into gym equipment, there was relatively little competition. The firm had gained from the massive growth in the market and it had also benefited from the fact that SMET was

one of only four companies in the UK capable of producing the full range of equipment being 40
demanded by the multitude of gyms springing up in every town. There were even fewer
manufacturers in the rest of western Europe and Emily was keen to diversify production into
France and Germany, which had become major markets for SMET in recent years.

It was for this reason that Jim was a little concerned about Emily's latest 'exciting plan'.
The cause of Emily's excitement was the new 'virtual reality' treadmill. Market research had 45
indicated that the idea would be a winner amongst people who wanted to keep fit in a more
enjoyable way. The R&D team had just completed the prototype of a treadmill that kept you
exercising whilst experiencing a virtual reality that could be programmed into the machine
— it had caused a sensation in the factory and workers were refusing to go home until they
had had their go. The invention had been patented, giving SMET a monopoly in the 50
production of this particular machine. Jim had also patented virtual reality exercise bicycles,
rowing machines and other equipment, in order to limit the chances of competition.

Emily had never had the same enthusiasm for the components part of the business — it
was difficult to get excited about such basic products. But Jim's favourite saying was 'Nuts and
bolts are the nuts and bolts of this business', and she knew that Jim would never stop 55
producing the goods that had been the reason for setting up SMET all those years ago. She
had argued, 'We should be changing the products that we offer, as a reaction to our different
markets. The degree of competition in each market affects SMET's ability to make a profit.
Should we still be making engineering components?' But Jim had always stood firm on this
issue. Consequently, Emily had worked hard to build up the fitness equipment part of the 60
business so that it now accounted for 60% of the company's sales revenue and 90% of the
profit.

A feature of the fitness equipment market had been the continued existence of capacity
shortage, in sharp contrast to the excess capacity that existed in the production of
engineering components. Market projections (Table 1) indicated that the situation in the 65
fitness equipment market would not change fundamentally over the following 4 years.

Table 1

Year	1	2	3	4
Projected demand for fitness equipment	100	120	142	166
Projected supply of fitness equipment	85	100	120	146

Despite this favourable situation, Jim had been frustrated by the firm's inability to
persuade the largest leisure company — Lloyd Davids — to purchase its equipment. 'It seems
like "unfair competition" to me: they buy all of their equipment from A1 Artefacts, the market
leader. A1 Artefacts produces a wider range of equipment than we do, and I've heard rumours 70
that it will refuse to supply Lloyd Davids if it buys any equipment from another supplier.
I guess that some gyms don't want to risk buying from other suppliers if it means that
A1 Artefacts cut off all their supplies. I must confess that A1 Artefacts' exercise bikes and
rowing machines are superior to ours, but I would choose our equipment in every other case.
Perhaps our new virtual reality treadmills will make them change their minds.' 75

(C) Issues, problems and opportunities

Leroy Winton spoke for the first time. 'As operations director, I'm worried about this expansion. We've had to make a lot of changes to the factory, to comply with health and safety legislation, and these have increased our costs considerably. I'm convinced that Magyar Metals, who've been taking some of our customers, don't have to spend anywhere 80 near as much money on health and safety in their factories in Hungary. There have also been complaints about unfair dismissals and redundancies in the components division, and the minimum wage, which we pay to all warehouse staff and machine operators, has increased our labour costs in the warehouses. There seems to be no benefit to companies from this government interference and I think we should consider a production plant in another 85 country. The Czech Republic's government is offering some very attractive incentives for firms that relocate there.'

'It's the consumer protection issues that annoy me most,' replied Jim. 'I can understand the government wanting to protect individual consumers in the High Street, but SMET sells all of its products to other companies — most of which are much larger than us. Surely they 90 are big enough to protect themselves!'

At this point Emily decided to change the subject. A key to her marketing success had been close examination of all of the latest economic trends. This had meant that SMET had been able to anticipate economic changes and plan accordingly. She waved a piece of paper in front of Jim. 'Bad news on the whole, I would think.' 95

It was August 2002 and the paper contained an extract of the economic indicators for July 2002 and a forecast for July 2003, published on the government's website. Jim scrutinised the summary that Emily had provided (Table 2).

Table 2

Economic indicator	July 2002 (actual)	Comment	Forecast (July 2003)
Unemployment	5.1% of the workforce	A rise of 0.1% since July 2001	5.5%
RPI	An increase of 1.5% p.a.	2001 rate = 2.0% p.a.	1.2%
Interest rates	4.0%	A fall of 0.5% over the year	3.5%
Exchange rate for sterling	A decrease of 8.0% since 2000		4.0% fall
Overall investment	A decrease of 5.4% in the last year		2.0% fall
Manufacturing investment	A decrease of 17.8% in the last year		7.0% fall

'Your summary doesn't mention the business cycle, Emily,' observed Jim.

Emily explained: 'The business cycle is in a slight downturn at the moment. The unem- 100 ployment is structural, rather than cyclical. By the way, it's 8.3% in our region — much higher than the national rate of 5.1%. There are worries about a recession caused by the decrease in investment and by companies cutting back on their stock levels. As you can see, overall investment has fallen, but for manufacturing investment the fall has been much greater.'

'Great,' said Jim, sarcastically. 'We're a manufacturing company!'   105

'True, but a very successful manufacturing company,' replied Emily. 'As long as we watch the economic environment carefully, I'm sure we can continue to be successful.'

SMET had been a success story in the 1990s, largely through its anticipation of the fitness equipment market. The company had been awarded the Queen's Award for Industry in 1996, mainly as a result of its exports into Europe, and added to its growing reputation.   110

EU regulations, which required consistent standards of quality throughout the European Union, made it much easier to export products to other EU countries. This part of SMET's business was expanding and exports had grown to 20% of its annual sales. The fall in expectations of inflation had led to success in reducing the rate of inflation, and this had helped UK exporters. In the late 1990s the high exchange rate had dented SMET's exporting 115 ambitions, but in the last 2 years the exchange rate had fallen.

Jim reflected on the company's success. With the virtual elimination of iron ore production in the UK, 100% of the raw materials used by SMET were imported, but only 20% of its products were exported. Consequently, the rise in the exchange rate had affected SMET differently from many other UK firms. Emily's training as an economist had helped SMET to 120 expand continuously throughout the 1990s and the early years of the twenty-first century.

The company's growth had not been without its difficulties, however, especially as the components part of the organisation had been declining whilst the fitness equipment division had gone from strength to strength. It had been difficult to keep the workforce motivated in the components division, and their colleagues involved with fitness equipment were always 125 reminding them that it was the fitness equipment division that was making the most profit for the business. Setting up reward systems that treated the two divisions fairly had proved to be impossible.

For 20 years SMET had been run as a private limited company, with Jim and his relatives as the main shareholders. However, Jim's original reluctance to move away from 'nuts and 130 bolts' had led to financial difficulties. The appointment of Emily, and her ideas to diversify into new areas, had been a condition imposed by the bank manager in return for a loan that helped SMET to survive in those difficult times. Jim had to admit that her arrival had transformed the business.

In the early 1990s, SMET had maintained a large sales force, all experts in metal manu- 135 facturing. This sales team followed up leads that arose from telephone enquiries from potential customers. Emily was convinced that SMET's sales force had lost contact with their market. She could find no evidence of any market research prior to her appointment and the sales force showed no signs of innovation or a willingness to take initiatives. Her first action had been to make the entire sales team redundant. Glossy brochures were produced and 140 7 months later a new sales team of supremely fit athletes was employed and trained. Sales of fitness equipment rose dramatically.

The need for additional finance to bring new technology into the business had been the key argument proposed by those shareholders and investors who had supported the move to become a plc in 1992. The extra finance available from shareholders enabled SMET to 145 compete with larger companies in metal manufacturing. More importantly, it allowed the fitness equipment division to expand rapidly. SMET had only survived this period because of the loyalty of its workers and customers. However, consultation with the workforce had revealed differing opinions. Some employees seemed to welcome the new technology, recognising the opportunities that it might bring. However, for other workers it seemed to be 150 having a demotivating effect. There had been widespread redundancies and Jim was not sure that the huge increase in profits had justified these job losses. A lot of his former employees had found it impossible to find full-time jobs since their redundancies and Jim felt personally responsible for their unhappiness.

Jim had always prided himself on running a firm which practised 'ethical business 155 behaviour'. In the early 1990s SMET had set up a number of projects that created new jobs in less economically developed countries. However, at the 2002 AGM there was despair amongst many stakeholders. It was revealed that some of these investments were supporting the policies of an unpopular dictatorship, whilst others involved deforestation of the Amazon and the extraction of non-renewable minerals. The argument that there was a conflict 160 between the company's need for ethics and the need for profit was not received with great enthusiasm. The Co-operative Bank, a major creditor, was even threatening to demand early repayment of its loans unless SMET could prove that it operated in a more ethical way. SMET's lawyers had checked the small print on the contract for the loan and, to Jim's horror, it confirmed that the bank could legally demand early repayment. But Jim wondered whether 165 the bank was behaving ethically in making this threat.

Sometimes Jim longed for the days when it had just been a family business. Nowadays, every decision seemed to be contested by somebody representing an interest in the firm. A policy that pleased the workers upset the shareholders; one that suited the customers was disliked by the suppliers. He concluded that it was impossible to please all of the people all 170 of the time, but there were times when nobody seemed to be happy with his decisions. He knew that Emily would be eager to take over the business, but he worried that she was too impetuous at times and needed a calming influence. Perhaps it was time to retire.

■ ■ ■

Paper 1
Macroeconomic opportunities and constraints

Answer all questions.   **Time allowed: 60 minutes**

(1) Explain the business significance of the retail prices index (RPI) (Table 2).   (4 marks)
(2) Explain the possible causes of structural unemployment in the UK's
    manufacturing industry.   (6 marks)
(3) Analyse the implications of the predicted rise in unemployment for SMET
    (Table 2).   (10 marks)
(4) Discuss the effects of the predicted fall in interest rates, shown in Table 2, on
    SMET's plans to introduce a new range of fitness equipment (lines 44–52).   (15 marks)
(5) To what extent have changes in the exchange rate contributed to the company's
    success?   (15 marks)

                                                                    Total: 50 marks

Answer to Paper 1: candidate A

(1) The retail prices index measures the rate of inflation in the UK.

> *e* This is correct, but not informative enough. The wording of the question means that the use and significance of the RPI is needed too.

(2) Structural unemployment is caused by firms becoming uncompetitive. In Britain, the coal industry is an example. It is also caused by a lack of demand. If people stop buying engineering products or fitness equipment then jobs will be lost in those industries. The solution is to retrain people or get other industries to move to the region where the jobs have been lost.

> *e* This is factually correct, but no explanation is offered for the first point and there is a minimal development of the second. The final sentence looks at solutions rather than causes, and so adds no value to the response.

(3) Unemployment will affect SMET in two main ways. First, demand will fall as people have less money when they are out of a job. If people are worried about their jobs (which they will be if unemployment is high) then this will also mean that they cut back on spending.

Luxury products are likely to suffer more of a cutback than necessities and so it is the fitness equipment division that will be hit hardest. Demand for nuts and bolts may also be hit if wholesalers and retailers lose confidence and decide to hold lower stock levels.

> *e* This answer is arguing logically and draws on the background in the case study. It is clear that the candidate is fully aware of SMET's areas of operation. Careful planning and preparation has enabled candidate A to apply an understanding of business in a relevant way.

It will save on costs too. A period of unemployment is usually linked to lower prices. Wages can be reduced as workers will want to keep their jobs. It all depends on the products that it makes.

> *e* The final sentence could have led on to more detailed analysis. As a starting-point it shows good technique, but the lack of any further comment means that it is not a complete analysis.

(4) A decrease in interest rates will affect the company in a number of ways.

First, it will make borrowing cheaper. This will make costs fall and lead to lower prices. If the market is very competitive, the company will gain a lot of sales, but for its fitness equipment (which sells on the basis of originality and quality) this may not be too important.

The lower interest rates will increase the disposable income of consumers, particularly those with mortgages and heavy borrowing. The relatively unique nature of the fitness equipment might mean that SMET could keep prices the same and just increase its profit margins and thus its profit. For the nuts and bolts it would probably be better if SMET used the lower costs in order to make its prices more competitive. It would depend on the reasons why customers buy the nuts and bolts. If they are more expensive anyway then it could be factors such as quality and reliability that attract customers. If so, then SMET would not need to cut price.

It would also depend on gearing — if the company is highly geared, the interest rate would affect it much more, but a low-geared company would not gain so much.

> *e* This response is not always expressed clearly but makes some good points which look at two key issues. The paragraph on borrowing is of a high standard, with evaluation of the nature of the product. The second argument is even stronger; the candidate is noting the possible consequences and acknowledging that a precise conclusion cannot be drawn from the information provided in the case study. The note on gearing is relevant but is not developed so well — AS candidates are not expected to understand gearing (but would receive credit if they used it appropriately).

The decrease in interest rate is only 0.5% and so any change is likely to be small for any of the factors looked at.

> *e* This one sentence demonstrates a sharp sense of awareness and excellent use of the data.

(5) The pound has decreased by 8% since 2000. This means, for example, that if the pound was worth €1.60 in 2000, it is now worth €1.47. This would make it much easier to export because a French person would find English products 8% cheaper and so they would buy English products rather than French goods (unless they really liked the French product). SMET exports 20% of its products and so this would not be such a benefit to SMET as it would be for a major exporter. In fact, SMET would not benefit overall because it imports 100% of its raw materials and these would become more expensive.

> *e* This is a superb treatment of the impact of exchange rates, with the application based on the information relating to SMET.

These raw materials will be 8% dearer than they were, so SMET's costs will be much higher than those of rivals who buy English raw materials. In England, the products will be 8% dearer and with inflation at 1.5% this is a big disadvantage.

> *e* This argument shows evaluation, but a question starting with the words 'To what extent' really requires some comparison to other factors if it is to be answered fully.

I think that this is the major reason for the company's success. However, it is not the only factor. Good marketing is needed and it says in the article that SMET has a good reputation and has won an award. These factors would have helped too.

> *e* The last paragraph does acknowledge other issues, but the answer would have benefited from some additional comment on their significance.

🖉 **Despite the first two answers, this script would reach the grade-A standard. In later answers the candidate uses the data well and the economic ideas have been developed logically throughout. The answers to questions 3, 4 and 5 are very strong. Ironically, the questions requiring lower-level skills proved to be the most problematic and would prevent the candidate from achieving a high grade A.**

■ ■ ■

Answer to Paper 1: candidate B

(1) This measures the rate of inflation. It looks at the price of a typical basket of goods each month, and works out how much prices have changed. For products with an elastic demand, price can have a major impact on demand, although if all firms operate in the same country, it is not likely to influence their competitiveness. For an exporter, though, it could make a big difference.

🖉 This is a very comprehensive answer that would earn full marks. It shows the value of clear language in achieving a full explanation without wasting precious time. The reference to elasticity of demand (from Module 1) is not necessary, but note how it has enhanced the quality of the answer.

(2) Structural unemployment is caused by changes in the structure of an industry.

🖉 Try to avoid referring back to the key word in an answer. The use of the word 'structure' does not show the examiner that the student understands the term.

If the demand for a product falls because no one wants it any more then firms will sack their workers. This is structural unemployment. An example is the engineering industry, as plastics have replaced metal products. Another example is when costs get too high and people buy from other countries. Britain used to make lots of metal products but wages are too high now, compared to places like Asia.

🖉 Effective use of language means that this reasonably concise answer would earn high marks.

(3) A rise in unemployment will affect SMET. Unemployment in the region is high and so it will pay low wages. A rise in unemployment will mean that wage costs will go down and make SMET's products cheaper and so it will sell more. However, it may still be paying higher wages than its competitors in other countries.

🖉 The candidate makes excellent use of the case study article to put the answer in the context of the company.

Demand will decrease, especially for luxuries such as treadmills and rowing machines. As people get richer they spend a greater percentage of their money on luxuries and so Jim's company might suffer. The export side of the business will depend on unemployment rates in the countries in which SMET sells its products.

e This response is a further example of effective use of the data. The answer reads well because it has not been memorised. The candidate understands the logic of the topic and is applying that logic to the situation.

In conclusion, I think that SMET will not benefit, because the decrease in demand will outweigh any fall in wages. Most of the costs are spent on buying the raw materials. Manufacturing needs machines (and is probably capital intensive) and so it may be that wages are only a small element of total expenses. SMET will make less profit.

e Drawing a conclusion is a good way of ensuring evaluation. However, the question requires analysis and so, in this instance, the final paragraph does not add much to the overall quality of what is already a good response.

(4) Lower interest rates will mean that it is less expensive to borrow money and so consumers will increase their spending. This will increase the demand for products and, as costs will be lower, it will increase profits.

e The candidate demonstrates sound analysis but no evaluation.

A lower interest rate will decrease costs because most firms borrow money or may have an overdraft. If SMET has an overdraft it will mean lower interest payments and so the company must decrease its prices. This will lead to a massive increase in sales.

e This part of the response is too certain. SMET will not have to cut prices and sales may change only slightly. Try to avoid exaggerating benefits (and problems).

The case study mentions that a part of the business was expanding. If the company has borrowed a lot of money for this expansion then the lower interest rates could be a major benefit. Such a large expansion may have come from more shares being sold or from retained profit. In this case, the interest rates would not have made any difference.

e The second line of argument is dealt with more effectively. The case study does not always provide concrete information on which to make judgements and it is valid to describe possible situations in which a factor becomes more (or less) significant. This answer shows high-level skills, albeit rather briefly.

(5) A decrease in exchange rates is good news for a company. If exchange rates fall then it will be much easier to export products and so Britain's balance of payments will improve. Companies will want this because it is good for the country.

e The point raised in the second sentence is valid, but companies will rarely consider their impact on the whole economy — they have more focused aims.

The exchange rate has decreased by 8%. This is a big decrease and may mean that the business will make huge profits.

e The conclusion is extreme. There is no context for this response and it seems that the candidate has left too little time to answer the question.

🖉 The quality of candidate B's answers is, in places, comparable to that of candidate A. The simple explanations (questions 1 and 2) are dealt with more effectively, and the answer to question 3 uses the data well. Unfortunately, the answers to questions 4 and 5 display weaknesses, and as these two parts account for 60% of the marks, candidate B's grade would be affected. Overall, the candidate's knowledge and analysis demonstrate good understanding, but no real judgement is shown and too little time has been devoted to questions 4 and 5. This candidate would earn a grade **C**.

■ ■ ■

Paper 2
The market and competition; governmental opportunities and constraints; social and other opportunities and constraints

Answer all questions.   Time allowed: 60 minutes

(1) **What is meant by the phrase 'ethical business behaviour' (lines 155-156)?**   (2 marks)
(2) **Examine strategies that SMET might use in order to benefit from a period of capacity shortage. (Section B)**   (9 marks)
(3) **Analyse the reasons why A1 Artefacts' actions might be seen as 'unfair competition' (line 69).**   (9 marks)
(4) **To what extent would the success of SMET be affected by the introduction of a greater degree of social responsibility in its actions?**   (15 marks)
(5) **Discuss Jim's view that consumer protection is not required when the consumer is a large firm rather than an individual (lines 88–91).**   (15 marks)

Total: 50 marks

■ ■ ■

Answer to Paper 2: candidate A

(1) Business ethics are a code of practice adopted by an organisation that is seen to be morally correct. This code is not based on legal requirements, but on what society perceives to be correct behaviour. An example of ethical behaviour would be a company agreeing to buy materials to help a less developed country.

🖉 This is a good definition, supported by an example that confirms that the candidate has a good understanding of the term.

(2) A capacity shortage is the opposite of excess capacity.

🖉 The candidate makes a sensible start. Defining the term overcomes the potential for irrelevance, which is particularly important in this case as excess capacity is occasionally confused with capacity shortage.

If there is a capacity shortage, a firm could benefit from low costs because it will be using its fixed assets very efficiently. This might allow it to cut prices and force the competition out of the market. I would not advise this strategy, though, because the Competition Commission might investigate if it became a monopoly (25% of the market). Besides, it will cut profits for a while and it does not need to cut prices to attract customers because of the shortage. It would be more sensible to keep prices high. In a shortage situation other competitors are unlikely to cut their prices.

e Although the candidate eventually concludes that price cutting is not a worthwhile strategy, discussing the possibility is a sound approach because it allows the candidate to display his or her skills. The critical factor is that the price cut is a *feasible* choice. The candidate shows logic in explaining why price cutting could be adopted, and then judgement (evaluation) in giving the reasons for not adopting it. A stronger argument is then added.

The company could also increase prices. There is a shortage in the market and only four competitors. This is a golden opportunity for SMET to make money before new firms enter the market. However, it does want to keep the goodwill of its customers and so this might be risky.

e The answer is further strengthened by the inclusion of an alternative strategy and the reasoning behind it.

I think SMET should increase its capacity. The capacity shortage is predicted to continue for the next 4 years and it should be able to sell all that it produces. This may enable it to dominate the market if it grows faster than its rivals. In the current situation it could be making a lot of money to fund this expansion.

e This is an excellent answer, earning maximum marks.

(3) 'Unfair competition' means that there is not a lot of competition. Sellers can fix prices and take advantage of the consumer by restricting supply or taking over competitors to limit choice. The consumer is not king.

e The candidate offers a sound definition.

I do not believe that A1 Artefacts' actions were unfair. It has earned its market position and the Competition Commission has the power to intervene if firms abuse their market dominance. The Commission has not intervened and so it must believe that the competition is fair. However, A1 Artefacts should not be allowed to refuse to supply products to a customer if the customer wishes to buy some products from a rival. This was allowed for some frozen foods where the supplier also provided the freezers, but it is unfair as A1 Artefacts are just taking advantage of its size.

It seems unlikely that a large firm, such as Lloyd Davids, would accept this unfair treatment. This could just be sour grapes from Jim.

Unfair competition is more likely to take the form of excessive prices or a cartel (and A1 Artefacts is certainly not linking with SMET in order to limit competition and take advantage of customers).

e A difficult question has been answered well. In real life, judgements on 'unfair competition' are very difficult to make because it is not always possible to know whether a firm is abusing its position. Lloyd Davids may feel that it needs to avoid upsetting A1 Artefacts, even if A1 Artefacts is not manipulating the market in any way.

(4) There is always a possibility of conflict between social responsibility and 'success'. SMET may have to pay more for raw materials if it limits its supplies to particular less economically developed countries. Consequently, it is likely to make less profit.

e This is a good piece of analysis.

Of course, there may not be conflict. Consumers who value this behaviour may pay more for a product that is seen to be helping a cause that they believe in. Mostly, businesses publicise their social responsibility — they do not want their kindness to go unnoticed. If SMET had a good reputation for employing local people, it would make the company popular locally and this would help recruitment, planning permission and local sales.

e This paragraph demonstrates evaluative skills.

In SMET's case, there has already been conflict when it made redundancies. It became a plc in the 1990s and now has shareholders who want it to make a profit. However, it is clear that Jim is not happy with policies that might save money by making workers redundant.

e The candidate makes good use of the case to answer the question directly. On occasions there will be obvious clues within the text.

The degree of conflict will depend on profit. When profit was low, SMET made staff redundant, as survival became the main priority. In times of high profit, the share-holders who want profit may not be worried by socially responsible behaviour that reduces profit, as they will be receiving good dividends anyway. However, if the market changes or the company becomes inefficient, then they might want more effort put into making a profit instead of supporting good causes. Few shareholders expect maximum profits. It is much easier to be socially responsible in a boom.

e This is excellent argument and development, showing the highest-level skills.

It will also depend on the competition. If competitors are not socially responsible, it will be harder to match their costs but easier to differentiate yourself. Are consumers interested in price or do they want a unique selling point? Social audits and responsible behaviour will not always cost a lot of money, and you may earn goodwill by doing something you would have done anyway.

e This is a full answer worthy of top marks.

(5) To some extent Jim might be right. Consumer protection was introduced to stop exploitation and this is more likely to happen to an individual than a large firm. If a large company is unhappy and takes its custom elsewhere, this will have a big impact on the other firm and so it will make sure that it does not upset the large firm.

e This is a good, qualified, opening paragraph.

However, I think that Jim is wrong. Everybody should be treated equally in a democracy, and it is wrong for a business to see one customer as more important than another one. Consumer protection laws make sure that this happens.

e The candidate is exhibiting a potentially dangerous style: is the answer going to stray away from business issues?

Furthermore, Jim is wrong because of the unnecessary expense that would take place. If a product is faulty, it means an inefficient use of the world's limited resources, and so this waste should be stopped.

e The answer stays just the right side of the divide between business analysis and other issues.

Jim has also ignored the fact that a dangerous piece of gym equipment might injure a customer of the gym, and so it will not be the large company that suffers but someone else (although the gym could be sued). In fact, there is a law that holds companies responsible for problems caused by faulty products.

It is very difficult to see if a product is fit for purpose, as described, or whether it is the correct weight or measure. For this reason, any purchaser is entitled to the same level of protection. It would be a dangerous precedent to set if firms thought that they could get away with poor products. It would not help exporters either, as I am sure that other countries would protect their large firms.

e The final two paragraphs are very focused. Overall, this is a good answer in which the candidate shows that he or she is applying understanding.

e **This is a high-quality grade-A set of answers. In the answers to questions 2, 3, 4 and 5, the candidate makes excellent use of the information in the case study, even though the nature of some of the questions makes this harder to achieve than in many other topics. The case has obviously been read and understood, enabling candidate A to answer the questions in context. All five answers maintain a high standard and the candidate shows good understanding throughout.**

■ ■ ■

Answer to Paper 2: candidate B

(1) Ethics means the style of management. It is the way in which the business treats its employees and customers, and whether it is morally justified in its actions.

e The candidate is guessing. This is not penalised because the loss of time is itself seen as a penalty. In this instance the last suggestion is valid, although too vague to earn a good mark.

(2) During capacity shortage a company would find that demand exceeds supply. This would enable it to change its marketing strategies and its marketing mix.

> *e* The opening sentence is sound — capacity shortage would enable marketing strategies to change (but they are not the only strategies).

The company has a unique product with the new treadmill, and could advertise this in health and fitness magazines, or in places like cinemas where younger people visit. Whilst it is new they could benefit from charging a high price, until 'me-too' products come on to the market.

> *e* The answer drifts away from the question, first by ignoring the reference to capacity shortage, and then by moving on to the new product.

The new treadmill could be made available in exclusive shops to help keep the price high. SMET could also charge higher prices for its other products. If there is a shortage then it will lead to a rise in price. It could also find new places — persuade new gyms to stock the products.

> *e* Only the sentence on shortage is relevant to the question.

(3) Unfair competition means that there are not very many competitors in the market. This makes it difficult for customers as their choice is limited. Oligopolists will compete by using promotion and advertising rather than on the basis of price and so goods will be expensive. With so few competitors, there is little incentive to innovate and so customers will not benefit from new products. Businesses may be inefficient too.

Oligopolists will also form cartels, to restrict competition.

> *e* The candidate recognises that unfair competition arises from markets in which there are few firms, but the argument is based on the market and not the abuse of limited competition. Only the last sentence is relevant and it is not developed. Most significantly there is no application of the question — it cannot be answered without reference to A1 Artefacts.

(4) There are a number of examples of socially responsible behaviour in the case study:
- Jim was reluctant to dismiss workers (although there were redundancies).
- The wishes of investors and shareholders (profit and growth) were being satisfied by SMET's expansion and diversification plans.
- The wishes of some (but not all) of the workers were met by the introduction of new technology.
- Pressure groups (and the Co-operative Bank) appreciated the support for less economically developed countries.

SMET appeared to be trying to satisfy the needs of lots of different groups involved in the business, but the case study shows how difficult it was to achieve.

e Evidence of planning and prior scrutiny of the case study is shown here, but there is no real explanation. It is not appropriate merely to state that the case study shows something. Specific examples and arguments must be used.

(5) There are many Acts of Parliament that protect consumers:
- Weights and Measures Act: this makes sure that companies do not sell less than they declare on the packet.
- Sale of Goods Act: goods must be of merchantable quality, fit for purpose, and as described. This protects consumers from faulty goods, or ones that do not do what they are supposed to do.
- Trade Descriptions Act: adverts must be honest and truthful.

e The final question has been misinterpreted, possibly because the candidate was expecting a question on the reasons why individuals need consumer protection.

All of these acts prevent companies from taking advantage of customers. This is necessary because it is impossible for buyers to know whether a product like a kettle will work until they get it home. If it explodes after 3 weeks, was it fit for the purpose? Consumer protection helps the individual against big business.

e Credit would be given for the full understanding of the legislation shown by the candidate, and the response would score on content. There would also be credit for the candidate's explanation and analysis of the needs of individuals to receive protection. However, the answer addresses only part of the question and no judgement is exercised.

Personally I believe that there should be no consumer protection. If people buy a faulty product then they should have checked it before buying. Any business that produces shoddy goods will not survive as people are keen to buy quality products.

e There is a danger inherent in having a strong opinion on a topic, as seems to be the case here. Evaluation requires candidates to weigh up the evidence and it is unlikely (but not impossible) that all of the evidence will point in one direction.

e **Candidate B has some understanding of the basic ideas, but this is often vague and so the answers are not always relevant. The candidate finds it difficult to put his or her answers into the context of the questions set. There is no serious attempt to evaluate in any of the answers. Relatively high marks would be earned for content, and some marks for analysis, but overall these answers would have just failed to reach the E-grade boundary. The failure to demonstrate the skill of application would make this response a U-grade, albeit a 'good' one.**

The everlasting sticky tape

It was the first holiday that Ricky had taken in 6 years. It seemed much longer. The flight to Hawaii was departing in 5 hours and Ricky and Gemma were sipping cappuccino in Alan's internet café. Alan had promised them a lift to the airport.

(A) The invention

Ricky recalled that fateful day, 6 years ago. During his chemistry degree course he had become fascinated by the 'sticking' qualities of different products and he had investigated the subject in considerable detail for his MSc. dissertation. At first it was just a bizarre fascination with stickiness that motivated him, but as his research became more detailed he discovered combinations of chemicals with unusual properties. It dawned on Ricky that there were business opportunities that could arise from some of the ideas that he was investigating.

The invention that changed his life was a substance that would stick tape to paper and wood. The unique quality of this substance was that once the tape had been pulled off the paper or wood, it would still keep its stickiness. His tests showed that it could be used again and again. The process seemed to be very straightforward and the chemicals and materials were widely available. Ricky was convinced that a large multinational such as 3M would already have discovered the product. It was 3M's 'Post-its' that had triggered his 'stickiness' fascination in the first place. Still, on the advice of a friend, he decided to approach the Patent Office, just in case. He could not believe his luck when the Patent Office told him that nobody had patented the process. Despite the chemicals and materials being widely available, Ricky was definitely the first person to present the idea of an 'everlasting sticky tape'.

Ricky registered his patent for 'everlasting sticky tape' immediately. He had also patented the 'unstick stick'. This contained special chemicals that temporarily removed the stickiness of the tape. On parcels and paper the tape was as effective as normal Sellotape, but once the 'unstick stick' had been rolled across it, the tape lost its stickiness. The tape could then be rolled up and within 24 hours would regain its sticky properties, to be used again and again.

(B) Business set-up

With a large student loan to repay and an overdraft, he was not in a very strong position to finance a new business. Ricky's father was amazed when he saw the sample that Ricky had produced and he agreed to provide some of the start-up capital. He also mentioned a number of his friends at the golf club who would back Ricky's venture, in return for a share of the profits. One had even offered a factory unit at a very low rent for a year.

Ricky had no understanding of how to run a business and was not very confident that his idea would succeed. Would people believe that the product could work? How was he going to market it? He had no clear ideas on the future and did not want to risk upsetting his father's friends. As a result he decided to start on a very small scale without any help, to test the feasibility of the business. For the first 6 months he operated from the garage at home in Bristol, producing batches of tape. The tape was transparent, like Sellotape, but Ricky did produce some variations of colour at the request of certain buyers.

The production process was fairly simple, but the small scale of operation led to very high 40 costs of production. Ricky wished that he could match the prices of the main tape manufacturers: his tape would not be more expensive if he had access to their flow production methods and scale.

Selling was the big problem. Leaflets were distributed to all of the homes in selected districts of Bristol, but very few purchases resulted from this tactic. Initially, most of the 45 sales had come from Ricky 'cold calling' local businesses. His original plan had been to sell the tape cheaply but to charge a lot for the 'unstick stick' that was needed to make sure that the tape was reusable. People were reluctant to buy the sticks and so Ricky had to offer them free with the first order of tape, and charge much more for the tape, in order to cover costs. 50

The first 2 years were difficult, and it was only Ricky's father's savings and his girlfriend Gemma's income that had kept the business running. After 6 months, the level of sales meant that the business had outgrown the garage. There was also a visit from the council, which insisted that certain chemicals could not be stored in the garage. Operating from a factory unit was more expensive, but Ricky received support from the Prince's Trust and within a few 55 months sales had grown enough to cover the increased expenses.

Ricky was still running the firm on his own. Meanwhile, his friend Alan was earning high profits from running an internet café. The irony was that this had been Ricky's original idea for a business, but the 'everlasting sticky tape' had seemed like such a good idea that he had encouraged Alan to open the café that he had planned to open himself. As Alan pointed out, 60 the café had been much easier to research and market. Ricky felt that it was the marketing that was holding his company back.

Fortunately, some of Ricky's father's contacts at the golf club had seen the potential of the product and become customers. This eventually led to a significant increase in custom, and Ricky's third year as a sole trader showed a reasonable profit. However, the tape was still only 65 selling to a limited number of firms, and to individual customers through some local stationery shops that had agreed to stock it.

The growth of the business now meant that Ricky had to employ staff for production, delivery and office work. These were parts of the job that he enjoyed least. Initially, the workers kept pestering him for help, but one weekend he sat down and compiled a list of 70 instructions for each job. This worked well, he felt, as he rarely needed to deal with queries any more. His instructions were very detailed and he was sure that they covered every possible situation. At first, one or two employees operating the tape-making machinery had questioned some procedures, but he had made it clear that his method was superior to their suggestions. He was glad when the two 'troublemakers' left the firm soon afterwards. The 75 new staff had not queried his ideas.

Ricky was frustrated by the lack of progress being made. He was now able to find more customers, but since handing production over to other staff, productivity had fallen sharply. He had trained all staff to operate the machinery, but they seemed to be much slower than he had been himself. People seemed to be so lazy and as soon as the bell rang at 5 p.m. 80 they rushed to the exit, even if there was a job that had not been finished. Staff showed no loyalty. He paid the highest hourly rate on the industrial estate and yet nobody had stayed at the firm for more than 6 months. It was costing a fortune to keep recruiting and training replacements, and he was always telephoning the agency to request staff to cover employees who had not turned up to work. Half the time the absent staff didn't even bother to phone him in advance. ₈₅

Ricky's accountant shared his frustration at the relative lack of success of the business, and encouraged Ricky to convert his business from its status as a sole trader. The accountant accepted Ricky's fierce desire to be his own boss, but with sales revenue of £500,000 per annum the accountant was determined to persuade Ricky that it was sensible to convert to ₉₀ a business that offered limited liability. Plc status would be needed to attract the funds and expertise to allow Ricky's invention to be produced on a scale that would allow him to compete with the price of traditional tapes.

Ricky was originally reluctant to heed this advice, being worried about the 'divorce between ownership and control' that tended to occur in plcs. Two factors led to a change of ₉₅ heart. Ricky suffered from a bout of 'flu, during which the efficiency of the firm fell drastically. This alone was enough to persuade Ricky of the wisdom of conversion to a plc. However, the second event made it a necessity, and again arose from outside the business.

(C) The breakthrough

The critical reason for the move of Ricky's business from sole trader to plc started with ₁₀₀ Cigarettes plc. The firm's headquarters were located in Bristol and it had been one of the first businesses to order the coloured tape that Ricky had offered. It had been the firm's 200th anniversary 2 years previously and it had purchased a large quantity of tape in the corporate colour — a very distinctive purple. It had not been cheap (Ricky had explained that this was a one-off job production rather than his usual batch production method), but the marketing ₁₀₅ department had been keen to celebrate the anniversary by using purple as much as possible that year, and so some purple tape had been ordered.

The managing director of Cigarettes plc was intrigued. The company had only placed a small order for tape but when he visited local businesses and friends he noticed that they were still using (or at least reusing) the purple tape. A telephone call to Ricky confirmed that ₁₁₀ only one batch had ever been produced.

With the future of cigarette advertising through Formula 1 under threat, Cigarettes plc was desperately looking for new ways to advertise. Within weeks the deal had been struck. In return for a 35% shareholding in the newly formed Everlasting Sticky Tape plc, Cigarettes plc would provide the factory and equipment for large-scale flow production of everlasting sticky ₁₁₅ tape and unstick sticks. Ricky received a 40% shareholding and additional funds were raised by the sale of the other 25% of the shares. The production line would be flexible enough to produce transparent tape or tape of any colour, but the standard, mass-produced tape would be purple and feature the slogan 'Smoke Cigarettes'.

Everlasting Sticky Tape (EST) plc was up and running. ₁₂₀

(D) The plc experience

Ricky also anticipated a market for other businesses that saw the tape as a way of promoting their firms. However, he was surprised to find that the other directors, most of whom had been selected by Cigarettes plc, objected to some of the requests received. Gun manufacturers and even GM foods had been considered to be unsuitable advertisers by his fellow directors. ₁₂₅

Ricky felt that this was hypocritical. Besides, he was a great believer in personal freedom. If people wanted to do something they should be free to do it. Ricky was finding it hard, realising that he was no longer in sole charge of the business.

At the first meeting of the new board Ricky was surprised by the huge number of items on the agenda. The first item was to confirm the company's key long-term corporate objectives. Only four objectives had been proposed: 130

- to produce high-quality products and excellent service
- to diversify into other products and services
- to support, encourage and develop the talents and needs of the company's employees
- to establish the company's reputation as a socially responsible organisation 135

Ricky pointed out that there was no mention of profit or growth, but was reassured when the other directors indicated that successful completion of the objectives listed would support other targets too. As a sole trader he had never bothered to decide on objectives — he had always been too busy to 'waste time' on writing lists.

At first, Ricky objected to the 'interference' (as he saw it) of the other directors, but after 140 6 months he started to recognise that there was a positive difference to the way in which the firm operated.

Everlasting Sticky Tape (EST) plc was proving to be a considerate employer. The facilities for staff were excellent, although the pay was now lower than in some rival organisations. Staff turnover and absenteeism were very low — staff appreciated the training offered by 145 EST and there was a pleasant working environment. The social facilities were excellent and social events were subsidised by the company. The money being devoted to research and development and quality assurance was huge, and the business was already coming up with new products to support the sticky tape. There was a real buzz about the place. Ricky, rather shamefacedly, admitted to Gemma one evening that he preferred working for the plc. It was 150 a much better employer than he had been.

There was a setback in the second year. The total quality management system introduced by the new plc had worked well, but a batch of below-standard raw materials led to the production of faulty tape for a short period and caused considerable damage to the equipment on the main production line. The compensation claims, lost reputation and equipment 155 replacement costs threatened the survival of the business. The firm returned to a system of quality control and checking but the damage had been done.

Conflict occurred at the second AGM. The other shareholders threatened a vote of 'no confidence' in the board if steps were not taken to give their needs greater priority. A partic- ularly vocal shareholder complained that the company was ignoring the needs of the share- 160 holders in favour of serving the needs of other stakeholder groups. The dramatic 70% fall in profit from the first year to the second year of the plc's existence had been presented as evidence of this neglect, and the directors' forecast of a loss in year 3 (until confidence had been recovered) provoked howls of outrage.

Shareholders questioned the wisdom of the company's four stated key corporate 165 objectives. 'What use are these corporate objectives if we cease to exist in the next few years?' queried some shareholders.

A compromise was agreed. In the next 2 years a series of short-term objectives would be established, with a greater focus on profit and new technology. After that, the original three objectives would become the priority again. Some shareholders became quite indignant at the suggestion that their interests conflicted with those of other groups, although two different views were evident. While some shareholders believed that the various stakeholder groups shared a common interest, others were adamant that this was not the issue — the company was there to serve the needs of its owners: the shareholders. Fortunately, the problem blew over and within 6 months reputation and profits had been restored. The forecast loss never happened.

The directors from Cigarettes plc were proving to be a strong team. Undaunted by the setback, they tirelessly sought new business opportunities. Their main challenge was to reduce EST's reliance on the sticky tape, and a well-funded R&D department was set up to achieve this aim.

Another strength was in marketing. The staff possessed a rare insight into changes in fashion and trends, and seemed to be one step ahead of rival companies in anticipating market changes. However, the variety of ideas was so great that it was not always possible to evaluate them fully. There was a real danger of overtrading.

Ricky had been an authoritarian leader. In contrast, the new team believed in empowering managers and employees. Full authority was given to managers to run their divisions, and they were encouraged to give similar freedom to their subordinates too. Ricky sometimes wondered whether they were given too much freedom. However, this arrangement did seem to encourage innovation. Once the quality problem had been overcome, the main role of the accountants became to find ways of raising the finance and providing the cash flow that was needed to support the continual flow of ideas through the company. This tended to be a short-term problem, as within a short time most of the new products were self-supporting financially.

Ricky had been lucky to set up his business in a time of prosperity. A period of upturn in the business cycle had led to major expansion overseas, especially in Europe. Twenty per cent of its sales were now in Europe, and the company was looking to expand into Japan and the USA. He wondered whether it was the right time to expand into those countries or focus more fully on Europe.

The marketing department had provided some forecasts for the next 2 years (Table 1). The plc prospered. It had been a steep learning curve for Ricky, but after 3 years as managing director of EST plc, he felt able to relax. Orders were now rolling in, and with a number of new products established, he felt secure enough to leave the business in the capable hands of his fellow directors.

Table 1

Forecasts	Europe		Japan		USA	
	1-year	2-year	1-year	2-year	1-year	2-year
Unemployment (%)	6.4%	6.8%	3.8%	3.7%	7.1%	6.9%
Inflation (%)	3.3%	3.0%	2.1%	2.1%	4.0%	4.6%
GDP (% growth p.a.)	+2.6%	+2.2%	+0.5%	+1.3%	+0.6%	+1.6%
Exchange rate: £1 =	€1.55	€1.50	¥180	¥180	$1.52	$1.60

Gemma's lifelong desire had been to go to Hawaii. When they had visited the travel agents they had booked a week in Benidorm, but without her knowing he had cancelled the booking 205 and substituted it with a month of luxury in Hawaii. He was sure it would be a pleasant surprise.

■ ■ ■

Paper 3 Starting a small firm

Answer all questions.   **Time allowed: 60 minutes**

(1) **What is the significance of 'limited liability' for a business (line 91)?**   (5 marks)
(2) **Briefly explain the reasons for the 'divorce between ownership and control' in a limited company such as Everlasting Sticky Tape (EST) plc (lines 94–95).**   (5 marks)
(3) **Analyse the reasons why the market research and marketing of Ricky's business might present a more difficult challenge than the market research and marketing of Alan's internet café (lines 61–62).**   (10 marks)
(4) **Evaluate the problems of business start-up faced by Ricky in establishing his business before it became a public limited company (sections A, B and C).**   (15 marks)
(5) **To what extent did the patents guarantee a profitable future for Ricky (line 21)?**   (15 marks)
                                                                       Total: 50 marks

■ ■ ■

Answer to Paper 3: candidate A

(1) Limited liability means that the shareholders can only lose the value of their shares. If a business gets into debt, its creditors cannot ask shareholders to pay directly. Creditors can force the company to sell its assets, but if this sum is not enough to pay the creditors then they (the creditors) will not receive the full amount owed. Limited liability encourages shareholders to buy shares, as they cannot lose more than their initial investment. Consequently, it is easier for companies to sell shares and expand.

🖉 This is a comprehensive explanation of limited liability, showing excellent under-standing of the term and its significance.

(2) The owners of a limited company are the shareholders. In small companies these are often members of the same family or friends.

Limited companies are controlled by the directors. In family firms these will be the owners, and so for most limited companies there is no divorce. However, as companies get bigger it is more likely that ownership is beyond the wealth of a family or group of friends.

🖉 The opening two paragraphs set up the answer well. In the second paragraph the candidate starts to explain the divorce.

These shareholders mostly want a financial return — good dividends and increases in share prices — and so they will want directors and managers who are the best.

This is not necessarily the people who own most shares. As companies get larger, the divorce increases. With over a million shareholders it is impossible for some companies to be run by their owners. Institutional investors (such as pension funds) buy shares but do not tend to vote at AGMs. They want the best managers to run the firm, but do not otherwise get involved.

e The candidate has done more than enough to ensure full marks for this answer.

(3) Small businesses cannot afford expensive market research and marketing, especially in the early years. They rely on secondary research through local papers and population statistics. Their marketing is probably word-of-mouth, or a small advert in the local newspaper, on the radio, or an entry in the *Yellow Pages*.

e This is a good introduction on which to build the analysis.

For a café this is likely to be enough. It will get its customers from the local area, and it will be very easy to see who and where the competition is. It may even be possible to note the types of firm that are closing down so that you can avoid that area of business. Marketing is much easier too. The target market is in your area and so local adverts can be used. Seeing how other businesses advertise will give the café guidance on how to promote. It might also point up methods that are not used and should be avoided. Niches can be spotted.

e This response shows excellent application to the scenario, with the candidate demonstrating judgement in the observations on closures and methods to avoid.

Ricky's sticky tape would be much more difficult. It has very limited local appeal and so his marketing would need to be national. It would be hard to persuade large shops like W H Smith to stock his product — besides he would probably not be able to produce enough. His rivals are very large firms, and they will be able to afford much better research and advertising. He was lucky that some local shops agreed to stock it. In fact, all of his sales have come from personal contacts.

e There is evidence of further analysis and application here, with effective use of the information provided combined with the candidate's own thinking.

As a plc, the company will be able to spend money to improve production. Another benefit will be Ricky's chance to market the product nationally.

e The final paragraph adds marginally to the quality of the answer, as the wording of the question does not prevent inclusion of factors relating to the plc. However, the comment on production is irrelevant.

(4) Typically, start-up problems fit into four categories: finance, marketing, operational and personnel.

e This is a useful start, as long as the points are then developed.

(Please see the answer to question 3 for the marketing problems.)

e Referring the examiner to another answer is bad practice. Never cross-reference answers — questions 3 and 5 do include some overlap, but the contexts are different. Question 3 is a comparison of marketing between two firms. Question 4 concerns problems of start-up for one business. An examiner will not look back to try to find a connection. If you think that an idea is relevant in two questions, you should include it in both, but be careful — this should be a rare occurrence in an examination.

Finance — small firms are short of cash and will find it difficult to survive. It says in the article that Ricky relied on his father's savings and Gemma's income. This means that the firm was unprofitable for a long time and would have gone out of business if he had not been able to get money somewhere else.

Operational — it was expensive to produce on a small scale. Buyers were probably put off by high prices.

Personnel — this was not a problem at first, as he did not employ anyone. Later on he showed poor man-management skills — he was very authoritarian and staff left.

e The finance section is covered well, but the other categories are not explained enough. Analysis means 'developing a line of thought'. The candidate has not really attempted evaluation but would have earned more marks for analysis by focusing on one or two issues and analysing them in depth, rather than trying to mention every area.

(5) A patent gives its owner a monopoly for about 16 to 20 years. Monopoly means no competition and so this should help Ricky to make a good profit.

e This is a good opener, but how does monopoly help profit? Sometimes students do not include logic that seems obvious. An examiner can only award marks for what the candidate includes in the answer.

It is not a guarantee, though. In the early years the tape lost money because it was expensive to produce and hard to market. A monopoly can limit competition and this helps a firm to charge a higher price. If the product has no uses, though, it will still not sell. There have been lots of patents that have not made money because they were not commercial (wanted by the public at a good selling price). There may be barriers that stop the inventor from breaking into the market. It would be very difficult to make a brand new car if you had no experience.

e This is an excellent evaluation of factors that could limit the benefits of patenting.

Another problem with patents is the laws protecting them. Copies are often made and yet the patent does not seem to stop this. In this instance the patent will not guarantee a profit. A slight modification may be enough to get around the patent, even if the basic idea is being copied.

In Ricky's case his father's friends at the golf club seemed to be important, along with his girlfriend's money. Without their help he would have failed. Luck will always play a part. The plc should help, but there is no certainty that it will make money.

case study

The patent has only been one factor influencing profit. However, it is better to have one than not.

e This is a limited ending, but a good observation that does address the question.

e **Overall, this would be a grade-A paper. A few marks would have been lost on question 4, which is much weaker than the others because of its limited analysis. But the other answers are of a high standard, so this paper would receive a good A grade rather than a marginal one.**

■ ■ ■

Answer to Paper 3: candidate B

(1) Limited liability means that the shareholders can only lose the money that they have put into the business. It applies to private limited companies and public limited companies. As a sole trader, Ricky would have had unlimited liability. He could lose his personal possessions.

e An understanding of the term is shown, but its significance is not mentioned. More than just a definition is needed.

(2) Shareholders are the owners of a company. They control the company by voting at the AGM. As owners they receive dividends based on the profits. If they think that the company is being run badly, they could elect a new board.

e This is a disjointed answer, suggesting that the question has not been understood. The candidate has explained a few key words in the sentence in the hope that this is relevant.

(3) Ricky's product would be very difficult to explain. Consumers would not believe that it would work and so they are unlikely to try it. The market research would have the same problems. Customers would say 'yes', it seems like a good idea, but would be reluctant to change brands.

e This is not the approach the examiner would have expected, as the question was intended to compare a local service (with a more easily defined market) to a nationally sold product that would be harder to market. That said, this approach does show why Ricky's product would be hard to market, so it is relevant.

It might be expensive to buy the special stick. Most people would not imagine that they spend very much on sticky tape and would not want to pay for an unstick stick, especially if they did not know the company's reputation. It would be useless if the product failed or the company liquidated.

e There is no comparison with the café, so this response does not fully answer the question.

(4) Cash-flow problems are experienced by most new start-ups. When you start you have to spend money on buildings, equipment etc. Suppliers will not give you credit because you have no reputation for paying on time. It is also typical for large firms to delay payment. A good business plan would have encouraged a bank to agree an overdraft, and the main banks have specialists who will advise and help small firms.

e This is a comprehensive opening, weighing up the problems against some factors that worsen the problem and others that ease it.

Ricky would need to set up a production plant and so he would need more money than a café, like Alan's. Location is also important. If located at the end of an industrial estate, then it may be difficult to find.

e This is rather naïve, given the nature of the business. The argument would be applicable to a café though.

If Ricky is the only worker, he would be vulnerable if he fell ill. He could not take holidays and his lifestyle could suffer. On the other hand, he does have independence. This is important for him and might override all of the other factors. If Gemma was in a well-paid job and he had large savings, then he could continue for a long time, but eventually this would be a problem.

e The candidate displays some excellent evaluation, drawing in issues of Ricky's lifestyle, personal priorities and his family circumstances and their impact on his situation.

Was Ricky a good manager of people? He found it difficult giving responsibility and trust to his employees. He did not take any holidays — this might indicate a lack of faith in his staff. If he does not recognise them or give them responsibility, then they will become demotivated. There are not likely to be promotion prospects in a sole trader business. Personnel effectiveness indicators such as productivity, absenteeism and labour turnover all suggested weaknesses and could have been fatal to the business. Fortunately, it had a unique product.

e The candidate is answering the questions using the background in the case. This is an impressive skill to demonstrate in an examination.

The finance would be the main difficulty; without it the business would go bankrupt. The other problems would just reduce efficiency.

e The comment on finance is valid but should have been better developed. It also lacks justification.

(5) Patents mean that no one else can make your product. You have a monopoly, meaning no competition. A monopoly can charge whatever price it likes and the customer has to pay.

e This is too narrow. The arguments presented are logical and correct, but stated in too extreme a manner. There is a lack of recognition of a whole host of other possible influences.

Monopoly is the best form of competition for a firm, and with a patent the government will not stop you exploiting the customers as it has given you the monopoly. However, with R&D it may not mean a profit straight away. Once the research has been paid for the business will do very well.

e The final sentence is good. Lack of time may have prevented the student producing a more balanced argument.

e **Overall, this is a grade-D set of responses. The answers contain no glaring weaknesses, but the focus of some parts is rather narrow. Question 4 is the best answer, showing the benefit of seeing the issues through the eyes of the person or people in the case study.**

■ ■ ■

Paper 4 Business objectives and strategy

Answer all questions.   **Time allowed: 60 minutes**

(1) **Explain why Everlasting Sticky Tape (EST) plc would wish to set itself certain objectives.**   (8 marks)
(2) **To what extent is it inevitable that the wishes of shareholders will conflict with the aims of other stakeholders in a company such as EST plc? (Section D)**   (15 marks)
(3) **Compile a SWOT analysis of EST plc and use it to analyse the ability of the firm to maintain its level of profit.**   (12 marks)
(4) **On the basis of your SWOT analysis, evaluate the possible strategies that EST plc could use in order to maintain its record of success.**   (15 marks)

                                                                            Total: 50 marks

■ ■ ■

Answer to Paper 4: candidate A

(1) Setting objectives will be useful to EST plc in a number of ways, i.e. to:
- provide motivation
- give a sense of direction
- enable the company to monitor progress
- assess the success (or failure) of individual staff
- improve communication

e This is a good framework for an answer, but there was no need to list all the points before looking at each one individually.

To provide motivation — if staff have a clear target, they will work hard to reach that target. This will encourage them to be more efficient and find better ways of doing their job. This can help the firm as it will have an innovative workforce. However, too much innovation may prevent the achievement of a target and so it could be argued that innovation is stifled by objectives — especially if they are very specific and quantitative.

e This is an excellent analysis of motivation and the answer has already earned high marks.

questions & answers

To give a sense of direction — individuals and informal leaders may develop in a firm and take decisions that are not in the interests of the company. It is doubtful whether Ricky was giving clear direction to the workers, as good communication is needed to guarantee a clear sense of direction.

> The observation about the change of objectives shows a high standard of evaluation. Full marks have already been earned, but the candidate is keen to continue. Questions that only ask for 'explanation' can be dangerous — there is a lot that can be said, but practice and discipline are needed to know when to move on to the next question. Candidate A does not have this discipline and is too eager to show knowledge.

To enable a company to monitor progress — objectives must be checked periodically to see if they are being achieved. In this way the managers can learn about their progress. If they are achieving their objectives, then the strategies and tactics being used are obviously successful. If they are failing to meet their objectives, then they can change tactics.

To assess the success of individual staff — if MBO is employed, they can see which employees are performing well. These may receive bonuses.

To improve communication — everyone will know what the company wants to do. Constant monitoring of progress will help everyone to understand what the company is aiming to achieve.

> Time has been lost — these ideas are not earning any more marks.

(2) Shareholders buy shares in the firm. If a shareholder has 500 shares in a company with 5,000 shares, then he or she will own 10% of the business and get 10% of the votes. Shares can be ordinary or preference — only ordinary shareholders get votes, with one vote per share. The dividend for ordinary shareholders depends on the profit made.

> This is a comprehensive explanation of shareholders, but more detailed than required. The question focuses on their wishes and aims.

Stakeholders have an interest in the firm. It will affect them in some way or other. Examples are trade unions (which will want good working conditions), customers (who want cheap, good-quality products) and suppliers (who want prompt payment). Shareholders are also stakeholders.

> The candidate has shown a good understanding.

It can be seen that different stakeholders have different objectives and this will cause clashes, but most will want a profitable company.

In the case study it seems that EST's main product appealed to customers, but quality assurance was a problem for a period. This problem was caused by a supplier of faulty raw materials. There was a possible conflict between customers' need for quality and the wishes of the supplier to cut costs and make more money. This also damaged shareholders who were worried by EST's falling profits. There will always be a conflict of interests between suppliers and customers, yet both need each other to succeed. If the product is popular and profitable, it will be possible for everyone to benefit.

e Good judgement is shown here, especially in the last sentence.

The development of employees seemed to be happening (training and facilities were excellent), although this was not true before it became a plc. Ricky failed to appreciate that bosses and workers could both have the same interests. The plc experience showed that conflict was not inevitable, although it probably seemed that way to Ricky in the early years. Conflict does seem to depend on attitudes to a certain extent. Ricky seemed to expect too much of his employees.

I am not sure that all of the customers would be happy with the purple tape. Personally, I would not buy tape which promoted cigarettes and would take my custom somewhere else.

The two main areas of conflict involved the managers. Ricky (an authoritarian) did not agree with the other directors at first. Personalities can often cause conflict, even within a stakeholder group. However, the main conflict was between shareholders and managers when the crisis happened.

In conclusion, I would not say that it was inevitable. The shareholders did not appear to have even noticed that profit and growth were missing from the list of objectives until a loss was forecast. At that point serious conflict occurred (but possibly only because of certain 'vocal' shareholders). However, once the crisis had ended, the conflict seemed to disappear.

e This response demonstrates excellent evaluation, initially based on the different wishes of the various stakeholders. The particular strength of this approach is its balance — it is tempting (and probably easier) to concentrate on the potential conflict, but the candidate has shown reasons for an absence of conflict. He or she has then provided a reasoned argument, evaluating circumstances that influence whether there will or will not be conflict.

(3) SWOT analysis

Strengths:
- beginning to spread risks
- growth and reputation
- mostly democratic leadership
- risk taking — innovative company
- financial success
- strong management team

Weaknesses:
- dependence on one product
- conflicting objectives
- link with smoking
- relatively few shareholders
- quality system

Opportunities:
- new markets
- GDP growth
- lower prices for exports
- support from Cigarettes plc

Threats:
- low growth in USA and Japan
- possible competition
- rising unemployment

> *e* SWOT analysis tends to encourage bullet points. Only content marks (3 marks for this question) can be awarded, as no explanations are offered. The second part of the answer has not been attempted.

(4) Building on its strengths, the company could continue to spread its risks by diversifying into new activities. The management team seems to be able to spot new opportunities, but it needs to be careful — cash flow problems can arise from over-optimistic expansion. Companies may be very successful during the boom periods but there are signs of slowing growth and a possible recession. There is a policy of autonomy which is a good strategy for growth, as it encourages innovation, but a lack of direct control might mean that failures are discovered too late. This happened to the quality assurance system, which was based on the 'right first time' philosophy. This strategy needed amendment and I would recommend more caution and greater control. Delegation depends on trust, but I do not feel that EST can risk another disaster. It will be harder to regain its reputation.

> *e* This is a solid start. The first argument is presented, analysed and then evaluated.

The policy of democratic leadership will be helpful, as it encourages more ideas — these will create new products and techniques that will help the company to succeed. The high profits being made will be useful in developing new ideas — this will be cheaper than getting a loan.

The company is exporting 20% of its products to Europe. Growth in Europe is forecast to be above 2% per annum — much higher than Japan and the USA. I would recommend concentrating on Europe. (It is possible that re-usable tape is an inferior good, and so a recession would actually boost sales. If this is the case Japan would be ideal because its economy has been stagnant for quite a while.)

> *e* This paragraph starts with repetition, but the arguments are relevant and indicate the candidate's knowledge and analytical skills, and some judgement is shown. Note how general knowledge has been used to add a well-informed insight at the end.

I would recommend that EST maintain its current approach to research and development. Product development is a way to spread risks — it is a problem if a firm depends on one product only. The company is already practising market diversification by moving into Europe. However, diversification costs money and can reduce economies of scale, so it is wise to keep it under control.

The main change that I would recommend is in evaluation of new product ideas. According to the case, this is not thorough. This could lead to unsuitable (and even dangerous, untested) products. Introducing a detailed system of testing and evaluation is vital; although it will prove to be costly, it should be cost effective if it helps to select the best ideas to be developed.

> The candidate puts forward another evaluative argument, again drawing effectively on the details in the case study.

> **This is a grade-A set of answers. Maximum or close to full marks would have been earned on most questions, but only a few marks on question 3. The answer to question 4 confirms that the error in question 3 was one of technique rather than understanding. This candidate obviously understands business studies but has been reluctant to curtail his or her earlier answers when there is still more to be said. Plan your time carefully so that you can recognise when to move on to the next question. Poor time management may have been the reason for question 3 being rushed.**

■ ■ ■

Answer to Paper 4: candidate B

(1) EST's original aims were not very clear. The company made a loss and shareholders were unhappy. The firm improved quality in order to help restore confidence and this ensured that everyone had the same targets.

> The candidate does not seem to have recognised the concept of 'good objectives' from the AS course. However, by reading through the case study carefully, he or she is able to apply logical reasoning to the situation and earn some credit.

Being socially responsible was a big disadvantage. It stopped EST from selling to certain customers.

The workers were treated well and their training would have increased efficiency and thus profit. I would need more evidence on labour turnover, productivity and absenteeism before making a judgement on how good the objectives were.

> The answer is not addressing the question. The general theme is the success (or otherwise) of the firm, but the answer does not refer back to objectives. Careful reading of the question would have helped the candidate to see that he or she is describing factors that may have helped EST to achieve its objectives, but is not commenting on the quality of the objectives themselves.

(3) SWOT means strengths, weaknesses, opportunities and threats.

> Candidate B has jumped from question 1 to question 3. Omitting questions is a potentially dangerous approach. You could easily forget that you have jumped a question by the time you have completed the question you are doing. Furthermore, there is often a logical structure to the questions, with later questions building on

earlier ones. If certain questions prove to be more demanding, it is advisable to modify your time allocation to allow more time for the questions that test your strengths. However, *in a paper where all questions are compulsory, it is safer to take them in order.* Fortunately, all questions were answered in this case.

There are too many factors in the case to cover all issues and so I shall just focus on the key strengths, weaknesses, etc.

e Excellent. It is much better to analyse a few points in depth than to spread your arguments too thinly. The mark scheme is designed to reward depth in one or two arguments as opposed to lots of different, briefly explained ideas.

The key weakness is the sticky tape. It is only one product and a company should not depend on one product for the majority of its sales. A sudden change in tastes or a major problem (such as their quality difficulty) could lead to disaster. There are also problems with the idea. If the purple tape is still being used 2 years later then will there be repeat sales? Even makers of durables such as cars rely on repeat purchases. If the tape is 'everlasting' EST will eventually run out of customers as the tape will continue to be recycled. It will be environmentally friendly, but a financial disaster!

e This is a detailed analysis of one key point and would be rewarded highly.

Fortunately, a strength of the firm is the fact that it seems to have foreseen this problem and is taking steps to diversify by spending a lot of money on research and development. R&D will allow the firm to understand customer tastes and so it will produce popular products that meet consumer needs.

e This is a good start, but R&D has been confused with market research and so the development is not relevant. This is a common area of confusion and you should be certain of the difference between them.

Opportunities and threats come from outside the firm. There is no real information on this in the case as no competitors are mentioned. Poor-quality suppliers would be a threat to EST's future.

e The candidate has not detected any external factors. He or she should have gone into detail on the supplier issue. More significantly, this answer fails to recognise that the economic information given in the case provides quite a detailed summary of opportunities and threats in respect of EST's overseas expansion plans.

Another strength is the financial backing from Cigarettes plc. It has put a lot of faith into EST and its marketing is also dependent on it, so it is unlikely to sit back and let it fail. The staff provided by Cigarettes plc have shown good management skills and this alone should help the firm to develop new and profitable ideas. The 'buzz' in the company suggests a place that has keen, motivated staff, and this will increase productivity and innovation and lower staff turnover and absenteeism. All of this means a successful business.

e The candidate has focused entirely on internal factors (strengths and weaknesses), ignoring (or failing to detect) the external factors. Would this be penalised? The answer is 'no'. The question does not specify that all four elements of SWOT are required, and as this answer is well developed and applied to EST, it would receive the maximum 12 marks. However, it is possible that a candidate may only be asked for one or two elements, such as just the opportunities and/or threats. In this case, candidate B would have struggled.

(4) EST is a successful business and should continue its present operations. The board is thinking of expanding into Japan and the USA. This would increase profit as sales increase. More expansion into Europe would also increase sales and profit.

Spending on R&D will also help profit. The firm has a motivated workforce and this will help them to maintain their success. The new quality control system will make sure that there are no further problems with quality. With a good reputation in the local area I would recommend that EST does not make any changes.

e The candidate has faced a dilemma here. He or she obviously believes that the firm is operating well and thus does not need to make changes. However, this is an examination and such a conclusion does not help the candidate to explain his or her reasoning. The above answer is really just a series of unsupported statements. It is usually safer to recommend (with reasons) some changes in strategy. If you believe the strategy to be correct, you must explain why you believe this to be true. Candidate B does not do this.

(2) A shareholder owns shares in the business. She is a part owner.

e The 'explanation' of shareholder is correct, but too brief.

A stakeholder owns lots of shares — more than 50%.

e This is obviously a guess, but would not be penalised and only a little time would have been lost.

It is inevitable that shareholders' and workers' needs will conflict. There is a limited pot of money in a firm and both groups will want the lion's share. Workers will demand higher wages and if they see that EST is making a lot of profit, they will be in a stronger bargaining position. It depends on whether EST could carry on making profit if there was a strike. If EST had a lot of stock or new workers could be brought in, then the existing workers would find it more difficult to achieve their aims.

e This is a standard analysis of the potential conflict. It appears that the candidate is just repeating an argument from memory because the case study provides no evidence of such a conflict at EST.

Workers will also want better working conditions, more training and longer holidays. All of these will cost money and reduce profits.

Shareholders want to make money from the company from higher dividends or share prices. Cutting costs will make more profit and, as wages are a major cost, this will cause conflict because the shareholders will want to cut wages so that more profit is made.

If profit is retained, the share price will go up as the firm is worth more money. A lot of retained profit will go into buying machines — this will cost jobs as workers are replaced. However, it will not always lead to conflict. Those workers who remain may have more enjoyable jobs (machines often do the boring, difficult tasks). The conflict will not be between the workers and the shareholders, but between the ex-workers and the shareholders. All the same, it may leave the current workforce feeling insecure. The loss will add to their insecurity.

e This is a more balanced approach. The potential for agreement between the two stakeholders is explored well, but it would have been better if the answer had focused on an issue from within the case, such as conflict between shareholders and managers over corporate objectives, or the quality problem that produced conflict between the supplier and EST.

Some people argue that a well-motivated workforce will make a lot of profit for shareholders because workers do their job well. In this case there is no conflict. Shareholders will want the company to spend money on the workers if it means more profit for them. Paying high wages should attract the best workers too.

e The answer could have been applied more fully to EST but, given that the term 'stakeholder' was not recognised earlier, the candidate earns some marks for content and analysis.

e This is a borderline D/E-grade set of answers. The first question is mis-interpreted, but some points are relevant. Despite the apparent failure to understand the term 'stakeholders' in question 2, subsequent arguments suggest some understanding and would be credited, but for content and analysis rather than application. Maximum marks would be awarded for question 3, but only a few marks for question 4.

ase study **C3**

Double D delight

(A) Digby takes a chance

The inspiration for the Double D theme restaurant came from a visit with friends to the local cinema. The Rialto was showing a karaoke version of *The Sound of Music* and, suitably dressed as Julie Andrews, Digby Dare spent an unexpectedly enjoyable evening singing along to the songs in the musical. The end of the film saw a mad rush as the audience tried to get 5 a meal or a drink to finish off the evening's entertainment. Digby wondered if there was an opportunity there somewhere.

His idea was a restaurant with a changing theme, according to the day of the week. On a particular night a karaoke film would be shown, projected onto large screens, and the diners would dress in appropriate clothing whilst enjoying their meal. 10

Digby had grown tired of his hotel job; his catering training had provided him with skills that were never required by the hotel's bland menu. Unfortunately, he could see no way of raising the necessary capital. It was at that point that he had a major stroke of luck.

He was in the hotel kitchen at the time the lottery draw took place, at least up to the time that the bonus ball was announced. The diners on table 4 never did get their soufflé. The 15 initial jubilation as he hurtled out of the hotel and into the nearest pub was tempered by the sudden realisation that he did not know how much five balls plus the bonus ball would pay. Fortunately, it was enough to set up the Double D theme restaurant. However, some detailed planning was now needed.

Digby thought that he had researched the opportunity thoroughly. Over a period of time 20 he had recorded the businesses that had opened and closed in his home town, observing the steady increase in restaurants and gift shops, but the decline in financial services and stores selling food and furniture. He had even carried out a survey outside the hotel that was located at the end of the High Street. He had been amazed at the number of elderly women who answered his questions: he was sure that the town had a younger population than his 25 research suggested, but he was careful to select every tenth person who walked past in order to get a 'random' sample. The results were depressing. Most customers expressed no interest in his restaurant idea.

For a while he investigated the possibility of a franchise, but although he now had the capital he did not like the idea of using someone else's methods. He was sure that his own 30 idea was a winner.

Digby was becoming depressed by the length of time that he had been unemployed and was even considering a job in his father's business. As a child he had been aware of the very long hours worked by his father, a farmer, and had vowed to seek a career in another industry. However, in recent years Jack Dare (Digby's father) had transformed the farm by 35 setting up Organic Pies Ltd. This organisation specialised in producing organic food (mostly pies) for local retailers. The setting up of Organic Pies Ltd had preceded the growth of interest in organic food and this had been a key factor in its success. Jack Dare had found that he was spending more time in the pie factory and less time on the farm, and was keen to persuade Digby to take on the role of factory manager. 40

Digby was reluctant to accept this offer. Organic Pies Ltd produced an interesting and varied range of pies, but Digby did not see much scope for job satisfaction. He had left the hotel because of its boring menus and he wanted to use his catering training to supply individual, high-quality meals for customers.

In the end, the decision to refuse his father's offer and open up his own restaurant instead 45 was quite sudden. A shop had become vacant at a very low rental in the next town and Digby bought the lease. He knew that he would enjoy running the restaurant, with its exotic, constantly changing menus and the party atmosphere generated by the karaoke films. He concluded that if he was enthusiastic, it might just succeed. All his friends visited on the grand opening, and from day one the restaurant proved to be both popular and profitable. 50

At first, Digby bought all of his food from the local supermarket. However, reading an article in the local paper about the problems of 'excess capacity' facing agriculture encouraged him to speak to his father about direct buying from local farmers. His father was only too pleased to offer his advice and gave him a list of local organic farmers. He even managed to persuade Digby to put some of Organic Pies Ltd's products on the menu 55 (although Digby was worried that this would damage his desired reputation for exotic, up-market food).

Digby was happy with the profits that he was making. The prices offered by the farmers had been very competitive, and a number of customers had commented favourably on the move to organic food. (Digby also noted that his restaurant customers were ordering more 60 and more pies, even though he had increased the price of pies twice in the first 3 months in order to encourage customers to sample other parts of the menu.)

Another benefit noted by customers (and promoted by Digby) was the fact that he was supporting the local community and providing customers with fresh, organic meat and vegetables. In the relatively rural area in which he lived the local people were concerned 65 about the future of local agriculture, and the *Evening Echo and Express* had featured Digby's new restaurant prominently as a supporter of the local community. This feature had led to a sharp increase in business.

Digby's second restaurant opened in his home town the following year. Over the next 2 years the business grew steadily, with more restaurants opening. So did Digby's difficulties. 70

(B) Difficult decisions for Digby

Initially there was sufficient money from the lottery win to finance the expansion plans. Profits were rolling in and Digby was able to open new restaurants (although he was now depending on bank loans to finance these new openings).

Digby's biggest problem was staff. During the period that he had trained as a chef he had 75 acquired a large circle of friends who were excellent chefs, and Digby felt confident that he could recruit these friends to work in the restaurant. However, there was a shortage of waiters and waitresses. This was solved by a recruitment drive at local universities and colleges. Desperate to pay off their loans or support their studies, the students were keen to earn some extra money. At first Digby paid them the minimum wage, but their productivity 80 was low and their absenteeism was very high. Digby solved this by changing to a piece rate system of payment. The high rate of pay per meal served led to greater efficiency.

His accountant was worried. 'Your ideas have been a hit so far Digby, but you're still operating as a sole trader. It's critical that you form a limited company to control all of your operations.' Digby was not convinced. He loved the feeling of independence from being his ₈₅ own boss, although he missed the excitement of the early days when he had worked within the restaurant. In the end, he reluctantly agreed to allow the business to become a limited company, mainly to keep his accountant quiet. 'Double D Ltd' was chosen as the name of the new restaurant business and his father, Jack, took a small shareholding with Digby owning the remaining 95% of the shares. ₉₀

Nowadays, Digby spent most of his time in the central office, issuing instructions to restaurant managers and organising supplies to the different restaurants. Originally this ordering had been carried out by the restaurant managers, but they had frequently over-ordered and this had led to a lot of waste. Digby had taken over all ordering in the central office and, based on recent trends, he would calculate the orders of stock to Organic Pies Ltd ₉₅ and the local farmers who supplied the restaurants.

Digby was surprised at his own character change. Before he established the business he had rarely got up before midday (after all, restaurant staff were busiest in the evenings). However, as the manager of Double D Ltd, he was always the first person into work, planning schedules and laying down exact instructions on how the office staff should organise their ₁₀₀ work. The staff had initially complained about the boring repetitiveness of their work but Digby told them that this was inevitable. During the setting-up of the office there had been time to send employees on external, off-the-job training courses, but once the number of restaurants had grown Digby had decided that it was easier to use the trained workers to provide on-the-job training for any new recruits. ₁₀₅

After a few months of high absenteeism Digby introduced a system of job rotation, encouraging workers to rotate jobs to avoid boredom. Digby also set up a bonus system where the hourly rate paid to the office staff was increased by a monthly bonus if targets for answering mail and organising deliveries were exceeded. Digby also spent heavily on the social club and encouraged the staff to organise social events. Ironically, their favourite social ₁₁₀ events were visits to Double D restaurants.

The rapid expansion of Digby's restaurants meant that Digby would occasionally need to buy supplies from elsewhere. The local farmers were finding it increasingly difficult to meet the demand from Double D restaurants, especially as restaurants were now being opened in other regions of the United Kingdom. Initially, Digby had bought supplies from another group ₁₁₅ of organic farmers but there had been a big argument when the managing director of this group had threatened to report Digby to the Competition Commission for 'unfair trading' because Digby would always buy food supplies from his father and his father's friends in preference to any other supplier. This worried Digby. Even if this was not unfair, was he acting sensibly? ₁₂₀

The business was a financial success, but Digby wondered if he could increase profitability by getting supplies from elsewhere. It did not seem logical that small, local farmers would produce the cheapest food.

He decided to look at three alternatives: continuing with the local farmers (including his father's pies), using a national wholesaler, and buying direct from ABC Farms plc, one of the ₁₂₅ UK's largest agricultural suppliers. Digby obtained some benchmarking data and summarised his findings in Table 1.

Table 1

	Local farmers	National wholesaler	ABC Farms plc
Index of vegetable prices*	111	95	90
Cost per pie (£)	1.30	1.35	1.15
Quality rating by customers#	9.8	8.8	7.5
Organic food (%)	100	90	50
Supplies deemed unsatisfactory by buyers (%)	2	10	3
Average delivery time (hours)	6	24	48
Late deliveries (%)	15~	5	5

* National average = 100   # Excellent = 10; Unsatisfactory = 0   ~ Increased from 0% in previous year

Digby decided to speak to his father, Jack, about the data — especially the increase in late deliveries. Jack was quite aggressive in his response.

'You like the flexibility of just-in-time, ordering food to be delivered within 6 hours so that 130 it is fresh and meets your daily needs. However, it makes it impossible for us, as a supplier, to plan our work schedules accurately. The factory and production line at Organic Pies Ltd are much larger than I'll ever need — our excess capacity is huge — although this is a problem with the whole of the agriculture industry. The rent on the factory is a drain on the finances too. I've got a lot of staff on flexible contracts but I don't get the orders from the 135 restaurants until the morning of production. This just-in-time system is fine for the restaurant managers. They inform your central office of the food they need the day before they need it and your central office sends the order out on the day that delivery is expected. This means that I've only got hours to sort out raw material supplies and the number of workers needed. We have to use job production then, especially with the pies. It also costs me a fortune in 140 stock control. Just as an example you can look at my stock control graph for chicken and ham pies for the last 10 weeks — you can see my problems.' (See Figure 1.)

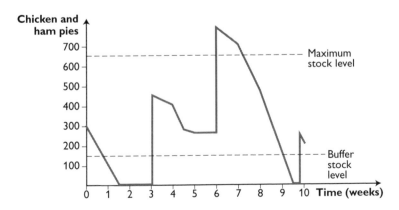

Figure 1
Pie stock levels at Organic Pies Ltd

Digby accepted his father's point of view. All the same, he was worried about the number of late deliveries. Were his restaurants getting too large to be able to buy from local farmers? Jack assured Digby that the spare capacity at the factory would mean that he could supply any 145 pies that Digby ordered.

'You're a significant customer for me, but most of my pies are sold to shops and I could meet any increased demand that you would require. However, I am not so sure about the other farmers. It would be easier for them if you agreed a long-term contract to buy everything that they produce. That would give them the confidence to plan an increase in 150 their production.'

(C) Digby plans ahead

Digby was feeling pressurised. He realised that he was trying to control too many parts of the firm and that he needed to delegate more. In his wildest dreams he had not imagined the level of success that he had enjoyed in the last 3 years. He was feeling overwhelmed by 155 events but felt unable to share the load. He was happy with the food supply — there were problems but he was sure that he could solve them, given the necessary time. It was the restaurants that were out of control. There was no planning. New restaurants were bought on impulse, as long as the cash flow allowed it. The early restaurants had all been located in towns which had a shortage of restaurants, but the rush to grow had meant that later ones 160 had sometimes faced severe competition, even from restaurants that had copied his idea and had set up a film theme restaurant before Double D had been able to open one in that town. However, sometimes the existence of lots of alternative restaurants seemed to correlate to high levels of sales in Double D restaurants. There did not seem to be a simple link between the amount of competition and the success of the restaurants, and Digby was at a loss to 165 explain this.

Larissa was the consultant that Digby's accountant had recommended. She went through the documentation far too quickly for him. Economic forecasts suggested a period of deflation in the UK. Had Digby considered overseas expansion? Unemployment was likely to increase, but not in the area in which his restaurants were situated. Had he considered 170 buying food from a larger organisation that could supply all of his needs, even if this meant ending his agreement with his father's company and the local farmers? Did he want to expand Double D Ltd into Europe? The pound had recently risen substantially against the value of the euro and other currencies, and she advised Digby to bear this in mind when making his decisions. The forecast was that the pound would continue to rise against the euro. With even 175 lower interest rates being forecast for the next 2 years, it might be a good time to borrow money.

Larissa laughed (rather unprofessionally thought Digby) when she visited the first restaurant. 'Why are you using these old tills?'

After some probing from Larissa, Digby revealed that he had decided against introducing 180 much technology into the restaurants and head office. The manual recording systems that they had used at the beginning had become so complicated that Digby had felt that it was too risky to try to introduce a new system into the business.

The most embarrassing moment for Digby was Larissa's request for the firm's corporate objectives. 'I've been too busy for that sort of thing,' he replied. 'At the beginning it was just 185 for my own personal satisfaction and independence, but the growth of the firm did become addictive. I guess survival is the main aim, but does it matter!' After 15 minutes of persuasion from Larissa, Digby could see that, after all, it did matter. He agreed to set down a series of long-term objectives and to seek the approval of the other managers for their implementation. After examining the firm's finances, Larissa advised him that any overseas 190 expansion would need to involve support from a much larger organisation, as the risks would be high.

The opportunity for support for European expansion was a chance affair too. A satisfied customer who turned out to be the Operations Director of Going Thomson plc, the leading holiday company, presented the proposal to Digby. Going Thomson plc would provide the 195 capital to set up Double D Ltd as a subsidiary of Going Thomson plc. Going Thomson plc would decide on the locations, which would be in Spain and Portugal. Digby would be given a directorship of Going Thomson plc, and would provide the staff training to ensure that the new restaurants would prove to be popular with UK tourists visiting Spain and Portugal. The UK restaurants would become part of the business and Digby would receive shares in Going 200 Thomson plc to match the estimated value of his Double D shares.

Digby's solicitor was an old school friend.

'The contract appears to be fine — I would say that you have a golden opportunity here, financially. The value of your shares is high, but you need to look at the wider picture. If I was you I would carry out a SWOT analysis of both your existing business and the new proposed 205 agreement with Going Thomson plc before you sign it.

'There are wider issues too. I think that it might be easier for you to resolve any potential conflict between stakeholders as managing director of your existing private limited company than it would be as merely one director of a public limited company, and so you should consider that too.' 210

Digby decided that he would read the paper before conducting his SWOT analysis. He turned to the financial pages to read about the Bank of England's decision to reduce interest rates. The Monetary Policy Committee had claimed that market forces had made it essential. Then his eye was caught by an article on the same page: 'IMF to restore fixed exchange rate system?' declared the title. It was an article based on a report from the International Monetary 215 Fund (IMF) which stated that the IMF would be consulting with its member countries. The spokesperson argued that the original fixed exchange rate system broke down during the period of high inflation in the 1970s. Lower inflation internationally now provided a chance to restore fixed exchange rates. The article cited the euro as an example of fixed exchange rates working on a local scale. 220

Digby was amused by his own reaction. Not long ago he would not have dreamed about reading such an article. Exchange rates had been something to 'investigate' the week before the flight to Ibiza, to see how much spending money was available for the annual holiday. Now he really needed to understand it because of its tremendous importance to the business proposal that he had received from Going Thomson plc. 225

■ ■ ■

Paper 5 Integrated Unit 2
(People and Operations Management)

Answer all questions.   Time allowed: **60 minutes**

(1) Explain the difficulties of just-in-time production methods for a supplier of
   raw materials (lines 130–142).   (6 marks)
(2) Briefly explain *one* benefit to Double D Ltd of off-the-job training (line 103).   (4 marks)
(3) Analyse the possible problems for Organic Pies Ltd that might arise as a result
   of the raw material stock control data in Figure 1.   (10 marks)
(4) Using the data in Table 1, and any other information available, advise Digby on
   whether or not Double D Ltd should continue to buy from local suppliers
   (Organic Pies Ltd and the local farmers).   (15 marks)
(5) To what extent did Digby use specific theories of motivation in the management
   of his business?   (15 marks)

Total: 50 marks

■ ■ ■

Answer to paper 5: candidate A

(1) Just-in-time means that the manufacturer receives delivery of raw materials just
before they are needed for production of the finished article. This gives a great
deal of flexibility to the manufacturer (or restaurant in this case) as it will not
have to store a lot of stock. However, it has the opposite effect on the supplier.
By having very short notice of delivery (6 hours in this example) the supplier
cannot plan production beforehand. This may mean that workers will not be
required to work if no orders are received (very costly for the business, unless it
can employ staff on zero hour contracts). If it does this then it will be harder to
recruit good staff. This could be overcome by producing goods to keep in stock
to meet future orders, but this could mean wasted stock (especially for food which
is perishable). The supplier's reputation could be damaged too if the stocks are
not fresh.

   e This is an easy question because of the clues given in the article, but it is unusual
   in that it takes the perspective of the supplier. The candidate has not been dis-
   tracted by this factor and has earned full marks.

(2) Off-the-job training uses specially trained experts to provide the training. Usually
it takes place outside the organisation. The main benefit is that it is provided by
experts and so should be of high quality. It also offers the opportunity to meet
workers from other firms, possibly sharing ideas and experiences. For Double D Ltd
the first employees used this training because there were no employees who
understood the process and so it was very beneficial. It also motivated the staff by
making them feel valued by the business — this should increase efficiency.

   e This is another focused answer that defines the term and then explains the benefit
   in the context of the question.

(3) The stock control graph shows some real problems. The most acute problem is at the beginning and end when stock runs out. To run out of stock twice in 10 weeks seems to be very careless. Given the excess capacity referred to by Jack it seems inexcusable that Organic Pies Ltd should be upsetting customers when it is capable of producing far more. Perhaps Jack is being too conservative and is more worried about waste than the effect on the goodwill of his customers.

e This is an excellent introduction, with (unusually) genuine evaluation in the first paragraph.

I believe that Jack's planning is at fault. There seems to be no pattern between the stock level and the time and quantity of stock received at the next delivery. A lack of careful planning is likely to cause further difficulties in the future.

Specific difficulties arising from the data are the stock-outs. If stocks of raw materials run out there will be no production. This would lose sales and damage the reputation of the business. The loss of goodwill would hit future sales as an unreliable firm would not be popular with customers. Digby seemed to tolerate this situation, but may not have realised that it was affecting his business. If restaurant managers were ordering food for the next day and it was not delivered, then restaurant customers may have become upset.

e This paragraph contains more examples of effective application. Instead of using standard arguments, the candidate shows how the effect could be passed on to the customer, who would also lose goodwill.

Production seems to happen every 3 weeks and so there could be a question mark over the freshness of the pies. Are they frozen to prevent deterioration? Are customers aware of this? Could production be arranged more frequently, especially if stocks are running low? The latest production run seems to be quite small — this could mean further stock-outs in the near future if Organic Pies Ltd has to wait 3 weeks for the next batch.

The purchase of the pies is unpredictable and this is causing most of the problems. On some days stocks are depleted quickly; on other days relatively little stock is used. This will continue to happen unless more regular production is organised. The other main problem arising from this is excessive stock levels. A firm holding high stocks will incur heavy costs.

Storage costs money in terms of renting (or buying) the space. There are also other costs to keep the materials safe and in good condition. Pilferage and damage are more of a problem with high stock levels. There was a real problem around weeks 7 and 8, with stock levels above the 'maximum'. Where were the surplus materials stored? Any temporary arrangements would have increased costs and risks of damage.

I believe that there are serious stock control problems. In my opinion, they arise from poor production planning. Jack should produce smaller runs of each pie, to make sure that the pies produced are fresher. There is also a problem that needs to be overcome. If restaurants and retailers inform Jack well in advance, then he can plan production more evenly. Thus I feel that the problems should be tackled but do not threaten the business in a serious way.

> *e* This is a difficult question. There can be many causes of stock control problems. The candidate has been careful to keep the answer relevant most of the time, and has produced a well-reasoned conclusion.

(4) The table does not present a clear picture. There may be significant differences in the nature of the products being supplied and so price comparisons may be unfair. There is also the difference between organic and non-organic food. It is more difficult and more expensive to produce organic food and so the table is again misleading.

> *e* The candidate makes a powerful start, with evaluation from the very beginning. However, it is difficult at this stage to recognise how important these issues are. It is usually more sensible to include comments such as these towards the end, so that their significance can be argued.

The local farmers are less productive (more expensive) than the other two suppliers for vegetables (but with pies the issue is less clear). Local pies are more expensive than ABC's, but this could be the result of different ingredients being used. There is also less food considered to be unsatisfactory by buyers from local farmers and I would rule out the national wholesaler on this basis — 10% rejection is a lot of food.

In my opinion, the answer depends on the nature of Double D's business, and there is limited information on this. If people are more worried about the quality of the film than the quality of the food, then price may become a more important issue. (The fact that they wanted more pies would indicate that high-quality food might not be top of the agenda.) However, if people use Double D because of the quality of the food, then price is not important. With the growth in competition, quality may become important — the films may be the same and so the restaurant with the best food should triumph. The prices shown are the cost to Double D. With a high mark-up on restaurant meals I would estimate that the final price of the meal would not be greatly affected by the different costs and so I would base my decision on other factors.

Double D will need repeat customers if it is to succeed. It has benefited from PR in the local press (based on buying locally) and comments from customers favour the organic food approach (and the pies!). With 100% organic food and the highest-quality rating by far, I would advise Digby to continue buying from the local suppliers. However, I would tell him to sort out the late delivery problem first.

> *e* This is a carefully considered answer. The data could have been used more fully, but the real strength lies in the appreciation of the limitations of the data and

the recognition that there are other factors that influence the decision. This is a largely evaluative answer, combining data and text in order to reach a reasoned conclusion.

(5) Digby used a number of motivation theories, although I am not convinced that he realised that he did!

The chefs who controlled the restaurants would have received job satisfaction from the independence, trust and responsibility that they were given. The job itself would have been interesting and given them a sense of achievement. All of these factors were recognised by Herzberg as motivators. However, the use of piece rate to reward the waiters was a hygiene factor — one that could demotivate if absent, but would not provide motivation.

🖉 The candidate gives an excellent introduction. Students tend not to link motivation to a particular theory and yet this is essential for a good answer. Virtually anything can be seen to motivate workers and so to show understanding of the theories it is essential that the theory is identified.

The payment of piece rate would be seen to be a motivating factor by Taylor. Digby also laid down strict guidelines on how jobs should be done, and this matches Taylor's beliefs too. Taylor seems to have influenced Digby's approach.

In the restaurants there was emphasis on enjoyment and a pleasant working atmosphere. Working conditions are a hygiene factor rather than a motivator, but they might have prevented dissatisfaction within the workforce. The party atmosphere at work is likely to have made the job itself more interesting and enjoyable — a motivator according to Herzberg. Job rotation would have made the job itself more interesting — another Herzberg motivator.

🖉 This is a good approach. Rather than building an argument from the actions taken by Digby, the candidate focuses on the relevant theory and then applies it to the case. This helps both analysis and application and lays down the foundation for an evaluative conclusion.

There is no real evidence of Mayo being used. There are references to central control by Digby. If this was true, then restaurant managers would have just followed orders, limiting the scope for them to feel recognised. The importance of teamwork, a feature of Mayo's theory, is not mentioned either.

🖉 The question asks 'to what extent' and so this paragraph answers the question as much as the earlier paragraphs.

In conclusion, I believe that Digby did use some motivation theories in his management, although I am not convinced that he realised it. He used Taylor's ideas fully and also applied parts of Herzberg's theory. However, as the business progressed he seemed to pay less attention to the theories. Digby became more autocratic, limiting the scope for other people to take responsibility. He also cut back off-the-job training, focusing on the less satisfying method of on-the-job training. He made little attempt to try to make jobs more interesting — not only would this lower the skill and interest level of the employees but it could also cause resentment by some workers and cause dissatisfaction. Overall, motivation could have been improved by greater use of motivation theory.

e This is a mature conclusion that helps the answer achieve full marks. The recognition that Digby changed his degree of application of motivation theories over time was particularly impressive, and demonstrates the advantage of being totally familiar with the case study.

■ ■ ■

Answer to paper 5: candidate B

(1) JIT production means supplying goods just-in-time. The major difficulties are caused by strikes with suppliers and difficulties with quality control. Materials are purchased and delivered straight to the production line, so if there is a quality problem it is not spotted until production has been completed. This can be very expensive to put right.

If there is a strike at the supplier, then the firm will have no stock to help it to produce or sell.

e The candidate appears to understand JIT, but fails to answer the question. This answer is written from the perspective of the manufacturer (the most usual view taken), but the question asks for the supplier's difficulties. Consequently, the answer is irrelevant, with limited credit given for understanding just-in-time.

(2) Off-the-job training takes workers away from the work environment and helps to motivate workers by giving them a feeling of recognition. Because the training is provided by experts, and often includes theory as well as practice, it is often more helpful to the long-term development of the worker.

There are disadvantages to this style of training. It takes employees away from the workplace and so production will be affected adversely. It is also expensive because the company needs to pay the training organiser, although there may be some government subsidies for training.

e This is a good start — the opening paragraph is theoretically sound, but there is no reference to off-the-job training's suitability for Double D. The answer should relate to the scenario. The second paragraph is irrelevant — disadvantages are not required.

(3) There are two problems shown by Figure 1. The firm runs out of stock — this could have been caused by a strike or a failure to produce at the right time. There may have been a machinery fault so that pies could not be produced when needed. It is possible that stock has been stolen and so the firm was not aware of the true level of stock.

The fault may lie with the supplier of ingredients. There may have been transport problems, although this is unlikely to lead to these long delays, unless materials were bought from another country.

The other cause could have been an increase in use. If orders increased, then pie stocks would be used up more quickly. This would have led to stocks running out.

e The candidate has not answered the question. This is a demanding question — there is less that can be said about the 'problems arising' than the 'causes' of the problem, but you must keep to the question. In the next two questions (4 and 5) there is potential for much more extensive answers. In this one there is less potential for a long answer. This will happen in some examination papers. The answer also fails to relate to the data provided.

(4) Food prices are much cheaper from ABC. Prices are 10% below the national average (and about 20% cheaper than the local farmers). The pies are also cheaper. On this basis Digby should buy from ABC.

The quality from ABC is much lower with a rating of 7.5. Local farmers produce the best-quality food, but the national wholesaler scores well too. A big problem with ABC is that 50% of its food is not organic. It might be possible for Digby to buy this from local farmers.

e This paragraph is too mechanistic. Although the data show cost effectiveness and quality, it is much better to draw on other evidence from the case to back up any conclusions, or to show whether price or quality is of vital importance.

A large percentage of the national wholesalers' products are rejected. Local farmers and ABC score well here. Overall, I would conclude that Digby should buy from ABC Farms plc, unless he wants 100% organic food.

e A brief, reasonable conclusion, but based on selective evidence. Tables of information rarely present a complete picture — the answer needs to connect some of these ideas to the information in the article.

(5) Digby used motivation theories a lot. Workers were paid piece rate — this would have made them work harder. Job security was provided and workers would have felt motivated by the success of the company.

A lot of money was spent on social facilities. This would have led to low labour turnover and a motivated workforce. A motivated workforce would have meant greater production, more profit and so more pay and so on to a happier, more motivated workforce.

Training was provided for all of the employees. This would have motivated them. However, a lot of the work was boring. This would have hindered productivity.

Overall, Digby seemed to use motivation theories more fully in the restaurants than the office.

e There is no evidence that any specific motivation theory has been recognised. The candidate just makes generalisations, based on 'common sense'. This answer could have been produced without any study of business studies and would therefore not receive many marks.

e **This script would be worth a grade U. Throughout the paper the answers are too vague, and this lack of clarity prevents any question from earning a good mark.**

■ ■ ■

Paper 6 Integrated Unit 3 (External Influences and Objectives and Strategy)

Answer all questions. Time allowed: **60 minutes**

(1) What is the business significance of 'excess capacity' in an industry (lines 133–134)? (5 marks)
(2) Briefly explain two factors that might lead to the Bank of England's decision to decrease interest rates. (6 marks)
(3) Analyse the potential for Double D Ltd to benefit from the use of technology (lines 180–183). (9 marks)
(4) Evaluate the degree to which the level of competition in the market affected the success of Double D Ltd. (15 marks)
(5) To what extent do you believe that Digby managed his business effectively? Justify your opinion with reference to the case. (15 marks)

Total: 50 marks

■ ■ ■

Answer to paper 6: candidate A

(1) Excess capacity in an industry means that there are too many factories. The maximum capacity of all of the firms in the industry is greater than consumer demand. This means that consumers have greater bargaining power and can force firms to lower prices or make special offers. However, with high fixed costs per unit this will probably make it hard for businesses to make a profit.

It also means that in the long-run less efficient firms or factories are likely to close down, causing unemployment in that industry. This will reduce costs, but also reduce the bargaining power of consumers as firms do not have excess stocks to sell.

e The candidate gives a full definition of excess capacity which also explains the business significance in sufficient depth.

(2) Interest rates are the cost of borrowing money. Although the Bank of England's MPC is responsible for setting the base rate, it must pay attention to market forces. If people are not prepared to borrow money at the rate set by the Bank of England, then it will be forced to adjust the rate. For this reason, interest rates are influenced by the supply and demand of funds. If savers are prepared to accept low interest rates and borrowers only borrow if they are charged low rates, then there will be a fall in interest rates.

e An unusual but very relevant argument that shows a keen insight into the setting of interest rates.

Inflation rates also influence interest rates. If inflation is low, then people who save money will find that their money has lost only a small amount of its value, and therefore they will only need a low interest rate to compensate. If inflation continues to fall, then interest rates will fall for this reason.

e This is another relevant argument which would earn full marks.

(3) Double D restaurants could introduce a computerised system. This would allow them to track orders of stock and enable them to monitor waste. Prices could be set by calculating the cost of providing a meal's ingredients and adding on an allowance based on cooking and waiter time per meal. This would help profitability.

The kitchen could be updated to include the latest equipment. Microwave ovens have helped kitchens to reduce the preparation time for meals and also to rectify mistakes made. However, although large restaurants can benefit from sophisticated kitchen equipment, there are not the savings and economies of scale available in restaurants as there would be in secondary production.

e This is a good opening. The strength of the answer lies in its application to the restaurants.

A computerised till system, combined with a loyalty card, would help Double D to benefit from gaining information on customers. This could be used to target customers. The existing system is inefficient and needs to be replaced.

The central office could benefit from technology. As technology has improved it has become possible to buy software that orders deliveries and plans schedules. This would allow staff (especially Digby) to focus on more interesting, strategic planning.

e Overall, this answer demonstrates a good understanding of the applications of technology to Double D Ltd.

(4) At first there were no competitors mentioned and Double D Ltd was very successful. Monopolists can charge high prices because there is no alternative and Double D Ltd would have benefited from the lack of competition. As Digby expanded into new places where competition existed Double D Ltd would have been in a situation of duopoly or oligopoly (a few competitors). In this market condition, competition tends to be based on promotion rather than price. In order to succeed, Digby will need to devote care and attention to marketing. His lack of market research to date does not lead to much confidence in the success of any marketing efforts.

This paragraph shows a good understanding of competition, with some use of the case study to apply the theory to the company.

Digby did not find any connection between the level of competition and the success of the restaurants. This may be due to the fact that there were more important factors influencing success. Specific restaurants may appeal to different individuals because of their menus, quality of service, or just the nature of the customers. In the case of Double D Ltd the enjoyment would be influenced by the involvement of the other customers, a factor that is not necessarily controlled by the company. Double D Ltd could be successful in a competitive market because its competitors can't cook properly.

 This is a relevant digression. The candidate contrasts the influence of competition with other factors that influence success.

The level of competition is difficult to measure. Would McDonald's be a competitor? There were two elements to the business — it was a cross between a cinema and a restaurant. When Digby saw *The Sound of Music* in the cinema, the viewers went to a restaurant or pub afterwards. Thus a cinema could have been the main competitor if customers visited Double D Ltd for the film rather than the meal.

The size of the market is important too. A place like London could possibly support hundreds of karaoke restaurants, but in a small town such a restaurant would struggle to survive, unless it attracted people from other communities. Transport links and car parking could influence the success too.

 The candidate presents two interesting arguments that are stronger on application than analysis.

On balance, I would argue that the level of competition was a factor, and certainly in some places competition seemed to limit the success of the Double D restaurants. However, other factors would be at work too. The quality of the competition was probably more important than the quantity. The same logic would have applied to Double D Ltd. Friendly staff and a skilled chef would have helped its restaurants to overcome competition, but even a monopoly would not survive if quality was poor. After all, you could hire a film and cook your own meal instead.

 This is an evaluative conclusion. Although there is little commentary on the types of competition, the answer meets the needs of the question in full.

(5) Digby's business was very successful, but I am not convinced that this was because of his skills as a manager. Identifying opportunities for business set-up is a vital management tool, and this was a strength of Digby as a manager. The themed restaurant was a good idea — Digby sensed that it would be successful even before he had the money to set it up. Perhaps more significantly he was able to identify further opportunities as the business developed. He saw the scope for modification of the menus to suit local suppliers and customer requests. However, after this initial burst there were no new ideas being introduced, and so Digby may have only possessed a limited amount of creativity.

e This is a well argued case, which supports the view that Digby's management was effective.

Digby's market research was poor. His sampling was biased and naive and his initial conclusions were incorrect. His original decision to locate in the next town was not planned, and the whole expansion seemed to be a matter of chance. Digby showed little sign of delegation, a vital management role. By taking on all of the main decision-making he stifled initiative and development in his staff, and reduced his own efficiency. His leadership style became autocratic, with no consultation with staff. Such a style is suited to emergency decisions but the only reason for emergency in Double D was the lack of forward planning.

e This paragraph shows good analysis of Digby's management and leadership style, applying theory in the context of Double D Ltd.

Digby remained as a sole trader for a long time. With unlimited liability this was a serious mistake — he even stood to lose his lottery winnings if the business failed. Although he eventually changed, it was on the advice of his accountant rather than his own planning.

The most serious defect, though, was the lack of any clear objectives. After 3 years of business there were still no aims and objectives, and even then it took Larissa's persuasion to convince him they were needed. It is difficult to see how a business could have survived this long without a clear direction. Digby was lucky that the nature of the business was easy to identify which meant managers and employees could see the needs of the business themselves in the absence of clear direction from Digby.

Digby's control of activities was poor. He had no idea whether he was buying food in an efficient manner, although he did eventually make a comparison. Even then he seemed to be basing his decision on family matters. This is not a rational business decision.

On the basis of the information, I would argue that Digby did not manage his business effectively. However, his original ideas were strong enough to overcome his managerial weaknesses. There were also other strengths that may not have been mentioned in the case. It is unlikely that a large plc such as Going Thomson would offer him a directorship if it did not believe that he had managerial skills.

e The candidate concludes with some excellent application, analysis and evaluation. Overall, there has been no attempt to try to balance the case for and against (quite rightly, because the evidence given does point to poor management). However, the conclusion is justified and the final paragraph adds a useful observation.

e **This candidate has given a series of excellent answers that would be awarded a high grade A. Some less predictable approaches have been used in places, but the individuality of the answers underlines the quality of the thinking. The ability to apply understanding to the circumstances of the case is a major strength in a high-quality paper.**

■ ■ ■

Answer to paper 6: candidate B

(1) Excess capacity means that the level of supply of a good exceeds the demand for it.

e This is a concise definition, but there is no attempt to explain its business significance. However, the definition would earn some credit.

(2) If the Bank of England decreased interest rates it would make borrowing more attractive. This would mean greater sales for businesses, especially those that produce consumer durables as people usually have to borrow money to purchase them. With low interest rates they could afford to borrow more. Mortgages would then cost less and so a typical homebuyer would have more money to spend at the end of each month.

Consumers might also save less (as savings would earn less interest). This would also encourage savings and so businesses would prosper.

If a firm has borrowed a lot of money it will find that its costs are now lower. It can earn more profit or invest in better machinery.

e A series of answers that, at first glance, appear to be fluent and knowledgeable. However, the points made address the consequences rather than the causes. Always read the question carefully. An irrelevant answer (such as this one) will score no marks.

(3) Double D Ltd would benefit from new technology. Machinery can improve productivity, lowering the cost per unit, so making Double D Ltd more competitive. If costs are reduced, it would be able to sell its meals more cheaply.

New technology can increase a firm's flexibility.

New products can be created by introducing new technology. New products can create niche markets or allow firms to produce a unique product. The lack of competition in such markets will help Double D Ltd to boost prices.

The case indicates that record keeping was inefficient because of the outdated tills. Modernising the tills would overcome this problem.

e The points made express some relevant ideas on how technology can influence a firm, but is the answer relevant to the restaurant part of the company? However, the opening three paragraphs are standard arguments and have not been related to the context. The second argument might concern the business but not the restaurants. Only the final paragraph draws on the case in a relevant way — limited credit can be given for the earlier suggestions as they could apply to any firm.

(4) The degree of competition will influence profit. In perfect competition there are lots of small firms all competing fiercely. There are no barriers to entry so new firms will enter the market if profits are being made. This will cut profits.

ℓ As in the previous answer, the candidate ignores the context in the case study.

Oligopolists will make more profit as there are only a few competitors, all with different, branded products. There may be some brand loyalty which allows higher prices to be charged than firms in perfect competition.

Monopoly means only one supplier. Monopolists will make the most money. With no competition they can charge whatever they like and the consumer has no alternative. The Competition Commission can investigate monopolies and stop them overcharging.

Double D Ltd is an oligopolist, with some competitors. This means that it would be able to make more profit than a firm in a perfectly competitive market, and so the limited level of competition will help it to be successful. In some towns, Double D Ltd has a monopoly and could charge very high prices.

ℓ The answer shows a strong grasp of theory and, eventually, starts to apply the answer to the case study. Credit would be given for content and analysis, but the application is limited to the final paragraph and there is no evaluation of the degree to which competition affects success. Some 'clues' in the text have gone unnoticed.

(5) Digby's original idea was popular with customers, and identifying a business opportunity is a key skill. He was also very astute in recognising the opportunity to introduce organic food and the popularity of organic pies. He was lucky that the local paper gave him good publicity. He was also lucky that he had friends and family with the necessary skills to develop his business. The lottery win was a huge stroke of luck — without this none of the events would have happened and so it could be argued that luck played a part in his overall success.

Although a period of deflation is predicted, Double D Ltd has grown during a period of economic prosperity. This was not planned by Digby — he merely started his business when he had the money available. I would say that he was lucky to be operating at this time.

Digby did not carry out much research. Only the first restaurant was researched in a serious way. The fact that all the restaurants succeeded was due to Digby's skill in identifying a trend towards this type of service, but he was taking a chance.

Overall, I would say that luck played a great part in his success, but that it was his skill that made the first restaurant a success.

This answer does not address the question set by the examiner. Instead it answers a question on whether luck was important to a firm. Make sure that you are not repeating an answer from a previous paper (unless an identical question has been set again). Because there was some overlap between the actual question and the one that the candidate appeared to answer, some credit would be given. The opening paragraph, in particular, starts in a relevant way, but the mention of luck seems to have diverted the answer away at that point.

The candidate has not always read the questions carefully. There are relatively few references to the case study and so the theoretical understanding of business (which is reasonable) has not been applied very effectively. It is possible that a lack of detailed scrutiny of the pre-released case study meant that the candidate was under time pressure in the examination, and made careless mistakes. No attempt was made either to draw conclusions on the evaluation questions. This paper would score a borderline grade D.

Note for students

It is advisable to study as many aspects of the case study as possible. You may wish to consider other questions that could have been based on these case studies.

For example, in Case study 3 there is a great deal of space devoted to Going Thomson plc's proposition, but no question set. A possible question on Case study 3 could be: 'Should Digby accept Going Thomson plc's offer?' Try to think of the relevant issues for questions (such as this one) that do not appear in the final question paper.